SIMPLE
SUSHI
COOKBOOK

OVER 100 ORIGINAL
STEP-BY-STEP RECIPES ∶ ∶ ∶ ∶
∶ ∶ ∶ ∶ ∶ TO MAKE DELICIOUS
SUSHI ∶ ∶ ∶ ∶ ∶ ∶ ∶ ∶ ∶ AT HOME

© Copyright 2023 by Sara Otagawa - All rights reserved.

This document provides exact and reliable information regarding the topic and issues covered. The publication is sold with the idea that the publisher is not required to render accounting, officially permitted or otherwise qualified services. If advice is necessary, legal, or professional, a practiced individual in the profession should be ordered. From a Declaration of Principles, which was accepted and approved equally by a Committee of the American Bar Association and a Committee of Publishers and Associations. In no way is it legal to reproduce, duplicate, or transmit any part of this document in either electronic means or printed format. Recording of this publication is prohibited, and any storage of this document is not allowed unless with written permission from the publisher. All rights reserved. The information provided herein is stated to be truthful and consistent, in that any liability, in terms of inattention or otherwise, by any usage or abuse of any policies, processes, or directions contained within is the solitary and utter responsibility of the recipient reader. Under no circumstances will any legal responsibility or blame be held against the publisher for any reparation, damages, or monetary loss due to the information herein, either directly or indirectly. Respective authors own all copyrights not held by the publisher. The information herein is solely offered for informational purposes and is universal. The presentation of the information is without a contract or any guaranteed assurance. The trademarks that are used are without any consent, and the publication of the trademark is without permission or backing by the trademark owner. All trademarks and brands within this book are for clarifying purposes only and are owned by the book owners themselves, not affiliated with this document.

FROM THE SAME AUTHOR

"Easy Bento Cookbook: 365 Days of Traditional Japanese Lunchbox Recipes"

The Easy Bento Cookbook is the perfect introduction to Bento box lunches for beginners who really want to dive into Japanese cooking, with both traditional and creative recipes, plus many helpful tips for getting started.

The high quality cookbook with over 100 easy-to-make recipes to create practical and delicious traditional Bento lunch boxes for your family.

BUY IT HERE
https://www.amazon.com/dp/B0BFFJHRP1

Or SCAN THE QR CODE with your phone

TABLE *of* CONTENTS

INTRODUCTION	**7**
Sushi, sushi, sushi...	7
The Exquisite Balance of Tastes	8
Sushi! A Worldwide Success	9
Let's Make Sushi	11
Sushi Varieties	13
Tools for Preparing Sushi	14
Focus On: The Makisu	14
Sushi Rice Preparation	16
Raw Fish Preparation	16
The perfect sushi roll	17
Focus On: Chopsticks!	19
Sushi Sauces	19
Spicy mango Sauce	20
Teriyaki sauce	21
FISH	**22**
Maki and Nigiri Sushi	22
Stir Fry Noodles with Shrimps	23
Maki and Nigiri Sushi	24
Easy salmon sushi rice bowl	27
Kanpachi Nigiri	28
Nigiri Special / Seafood medley	29
California Roll Sushi	30
Crab and avocado sushi	31
Crab stick salad canapé	31
Simple Smoked Salmon Sushi	32
New York Roll / Shrimp, avocado, cucumber	33
Tuna Delight Nigiri	34
Brown rice smoked salmon rolls	35
Marinated Tuna Hand Rolls	36

Sushi Spaghetti Salad	37
Cocktail sushi	38
Crab stick salad canapé	39
Salmon Roe Canapé	39
Cream Cheese & Crab Rolls	40
Cucumber sushi parcels + salmon	41
Curry Salmon Sushi Stacks	42
Grilled eel sushi	43
Inside-Out Spicy Tuna & Avo Sushi	44
Japanese omelet sushi	45
Cauliflower Tuna Sushi Rolls	46
Maki Sushi with Baked Fish	47
Mango & Curry Salmon Stacks + Rice	48
Marinated Fish Sushi	49
Full Sea Sushi	50
Paella Sushi	51
Rice & Quinoa Prawn Sushi Bowl	52
Restaurant-style Raw Fish Sushi	53
Salmon Sushi Salad	54
Shrimp and Salmon Sushi Rolls	55
Spicy Tuna Sesame Roll	57
Shrimp Rice Pilaf Sushi	58
Shrimp Rolls	59
Shrimp Sushi	60
Smoked Mackerel Maki Rolls	61
Smoked Salmon Canapé	62
soft-Shell Crab Sushi Roll	62
Smoked Salmon Sushi Roll	63
Spicy Crab Roll	64
Tuna Avocado Sushi Rice Salad	65
Spicy Tuna Sushi Roll	66
Sushi Crab Salad Recipe	67
Sushi Eel Eggrolls w/ Cream Cheese	68
Thai Shrimp Sushi Parcels	69
Tokyo-style Sushi Rice Salad	70

Traditional Nori Tuna Rolls	71
Tuna Salad Rolls	72
Tuna Fillet Rice Salad	73
Tuna Tartare Gunkan Sushi	74
Two-cheese Tuna Salad Rolls	75

MEAT 76

Barbecued pork inside-out rolls	76
Barbecue Hot Dog Sushi Roll	77
Beef celery sushi rice salad	78
Buffalo Chicken Sushi	79
Chicken rice sushi	80
Chicken Salad Sushi	81
Chicken Sushi	82
Grilled Bacon Sushi Roll	83
Korean Kimchi Sushi Rolls	84
Onigirazu	85
Green Sushi w/ Fresh Goat Cheese	87
Peking Duck Sushi	88
Pink Sushi	89
Pork Cutlet Tonkatsu Sushi	90
Smoked Duck Sushi w/ Orange	91
Prosciutto Rolls	92
Roast Beef Asparagus Rolls	93
Seared Tataki Beef Sushi	94
Original Mushroom and Chicken Sushi Rice	95
Sweet Chili Chicken Sushi	96
Taco sushi	97
Teriyaki Chicken Pouches Sushi	98
Teriyaki Chicken Sushi Roll	99
Chicken Sushi Delicacy	100
Chili Rice Bowl with Beef & Egg	101
Yakitori Sushi Skewers	102

VEGETARIAN 104

Veggie Sushi	103
Cucumber Sushi Rolls	104
Butternut Squash Rolls	105
Vegan Sushi Bowls	106
Brown Rice Quinoa Sushi Rolls	107
Cauliflower Rice Sushi Bowls	108
Cauliflower Rice Sushi Bowls with Tofu	109
Chickpea Salad Sushi Wrap	110
Crispy Tofu Sushi Burrito	111
Stir Fry Noodles with Shrimps	112
Vegan Sushi Burrito w/ Air Fryer Tofu	113
Furikake Sushi Casserole	114
Eggplant sushi	115
Homemade Vegan Sushi Rolls + Quinoa	117
Mango Sushi Bowl	118
Quinoa Sushi Rolls w/	119
Miso-Sesame Dipping Sauce	119
Sushi Burrito Bowl	120
Roasted Sweet Potato Sushi	121
Sweet Potato Tempura & Avocado Rolls	122
Tofu & Mushroom Kimbap Wrap	124
Vegan Sushi Bowl w/ Sesame Soy Dressing	125
Vegan Sushi Sandwich	126

DESSERTS & SPECIALS 128

Fruit Sushi Rice	127
Fig & Coconut Dessert Sushi	128
Sweet Sushi with Chocolate	129
Sweet Sushi w/ Kiwi Rhubarb	130
Key Lime Dessert Sushi	131
Cocktail sushi	132

CONCLUSION 133
INDEX 134

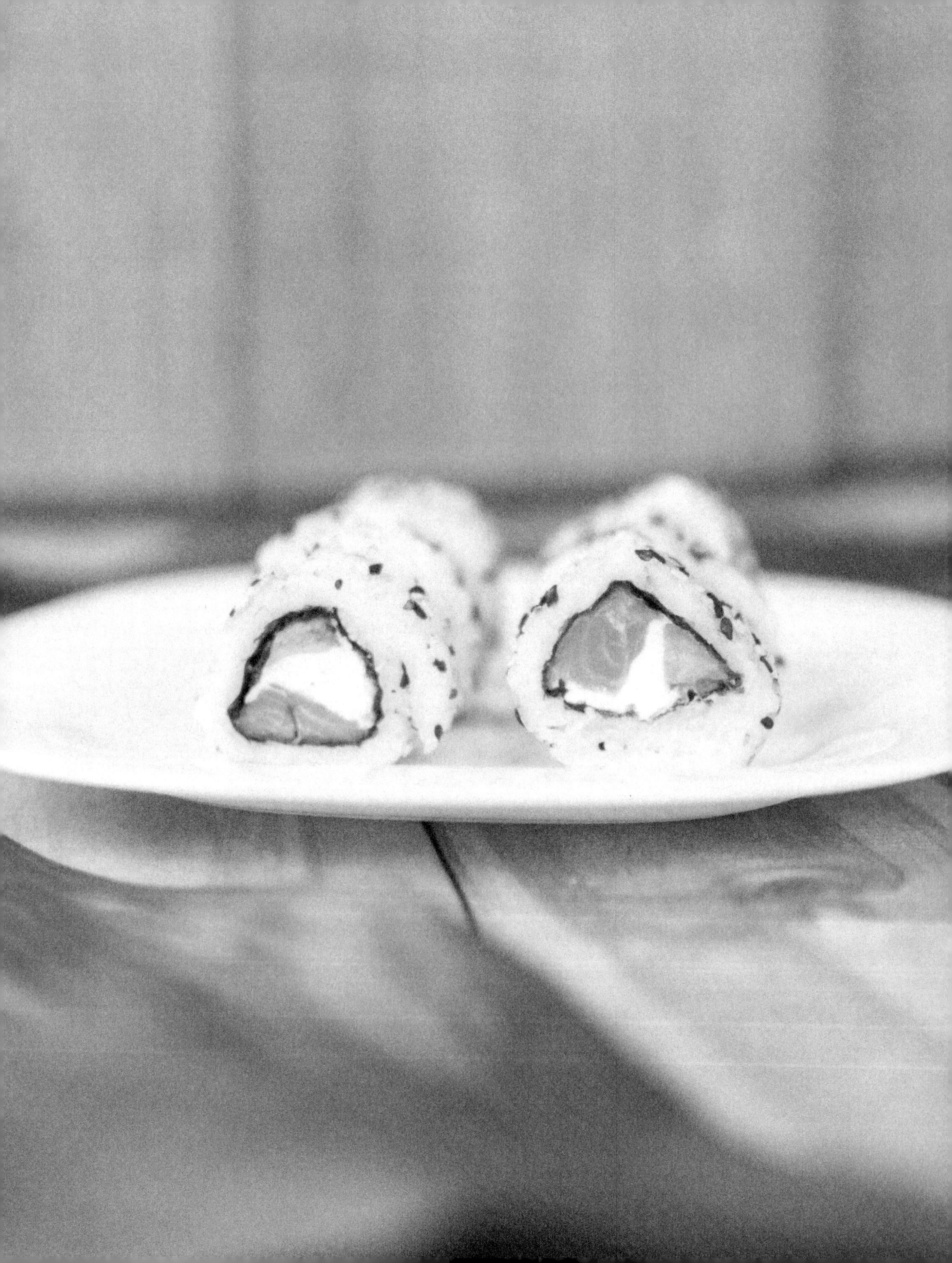

INTRODUCTION
To The Sushi Cookbook

SUSHI, SUSHI, SUSHI...

After the success of my first book on Bentos, I've been lucky enough to have had many requests to follow up with other books focusing on other aspects and kinds of specialties of Japanese cooking.

The first book was written out of passion and of being a mom and "family manager" with the practical solutions that quick box lunches could give to someone in my same situation (you can check The Easy Bento Cookbook at this link *https://www.amazon.com/dp/B0BFHVHW7D*, or scan the QR code somewhere in the first pages of this book).

The vast majority of the feedback I've got on my social media was to ask to put out there my contribution to what is without a doubt the most illustrious and successful representative of Japanese culinary culture in the world: Sushi!
Sushi is such a cultural Japanese treasure guarded by legendary chefs that crafted the art for thousands of years that often times the prospect of cooking some at home can be intimidating. Nothing could be farther from the truth.

Sushi was born as a simple food, to concentrate food freshness, quality, and taste in small nutritious bites. That's why sushi preparation is accessible to everybody.

Making sushi is actually very easy.
Gather the freshest ingredients, a few tools you already have in your kitchen, a bit of practice, and you're set to prepare delicious sushi. Within the pages of this book, I'll show you exactly how.

I am sure you will enjoy this journey into Japanese cuisine and sushi knowledge. You will find my version of all the classics, plus some original and surprising recipes with meat and vegetables!
I can't wait to hear your feedback on the delicious sushi you that you will be able to prepare very soon.

Sarah

JAPANESE CUISINE: THE EXQUISITE BALANCE OF TASTES

Japanese cuisine is a culinary tradition that is known for its simplicity, attention to detail, and use of fresh ingredients. These traits are evident in many aspects of Japanese cooking, and they have contributed to the popularity and widespread appeal of Japanese food.

One of the main traits of Japanese cuisine is its focus on simplicity. Japanese cooks strive to let the natural flavors of the ingredients shine, rather than masking them with heavy sauces or complex spice blends. This is achieved through techniques such as grilling, steaming, and boiling, which help to bring out the natural flavors of the ingredients.

A key trait of Japanese cuisine that reveal the core values of it culture is the attentive attention to detail that goes into every dish. From the presentation of the food to the way it is cooked, Japanese cooks take great care to ensure that every aspect of the dish is flawless. This attention to detail is evident in the precise cuts of the ingredients, the arrangement of the food on the plate, and the use of garnishes and other decorative touches.

Freshness is also a key trait of Japanese culinary culture. Japanese cooks place a high value on using ingredients that are at the peak of their seasonality, as they believe that this helps to ensure the best flavor and quality of the dish. That's why using fresh and locally available seafood, vegetables, and fruits is fundamental for a master Japanese chef.

In addition to these main traits, Japanese cuisine is also known for its use of a wide range of ingredients and cooking techniques. These include the use of soy sauce, miso, sake, and mirin, as well as the use of traditional cooking methods such as tempura, teriyaki, and shabu-shabu.

So we can say that the main traits of Japanese cuisine are simplicity, attention to detail, and the use of fresh ingredients. These characteristics, combined with a wide range of ingredients and cooking techniques, have contributed to the popularity and enduring appeal of Japanese food.

Simplicity though, is a surface trait that resulted from a very ancient tradition, where layers of history, people, cultures and events slowly made what is Japanese cooking today.

As you peel though these layers you'll find that Japanese cuisine is a multifaceted and sophisticated culinary tradition that has developed over thousands of years. Of all traditions, in this book we will focus on Sushi, that is perhaps one of the most well-known and beloved aspects of Japanese cuisine, and it has a rich history and cultural significance that continues to this day.

SUSHI!
A WORLDWIDE SUCCESS

In Japan, sushi has a special place in people's hearts. It's not just a mainstay of Japanese culture, but it's also become a mainstay of contemporary culinary fare. Sushi has gone from regular cuisine to the most popular in decades. On the other hand, sushi in Japan is more than simply a simple cuisine; it expresses their past. Sushi isn't an old meal, but it has a lot of cultural significance.

Throughout Japanese history, sushi has played a significant role. Hot dogs in the United States may have anything to do with this phenomenon. Many people associate hamburgers & hot dogs with the United States and how they are ingrained in American society. On the other hand, sushi may be seen in the same manner. In Japan, it's a way of life.

The sushi business has also contributed to the development of Japan as a country. Located in Japan is the Tsukiji fish market, the world's most important fish market. Approximately 5.6 billion dollars worth of seafood is sold each year. Approximately 600 billion yen is involved. Sushi has played a significant role in elevating Japan from its former status as a mostly isolated nation to one that is now a global player: because of the increasing popularity of sushi across the world, Japan has emerged as a major player in the worldwide fish trade. Neither will be conceivable in the absence of sushi's global appeal and Japan's technological advances.

In addition to its historical and cultural significance in Japan, sushi has had a significant role in determining the current state of the global food industry. Without the advancements in contemporary food globalization and transportation, sushi may not have been as popular as it is now. Tuna fish plays a big role in this. Because of its high-fat content, tuna used to be shunned by many Japanese diners. However, when the Japanese developed a taste for the fatty tuna parts known as toro, global demand for the fish increased. Fishermen had to adjust to the shifting market conditions as a result. More fish have to be captured to meet the increasing demand for tuna. Fishermen must return to the beach promptly after a big haul of tuna to process it since the fish degrades fast, so new technologies were required to fulfill the rising demand for tuna to enable fishermen to remain out longer and capture more of the fish.

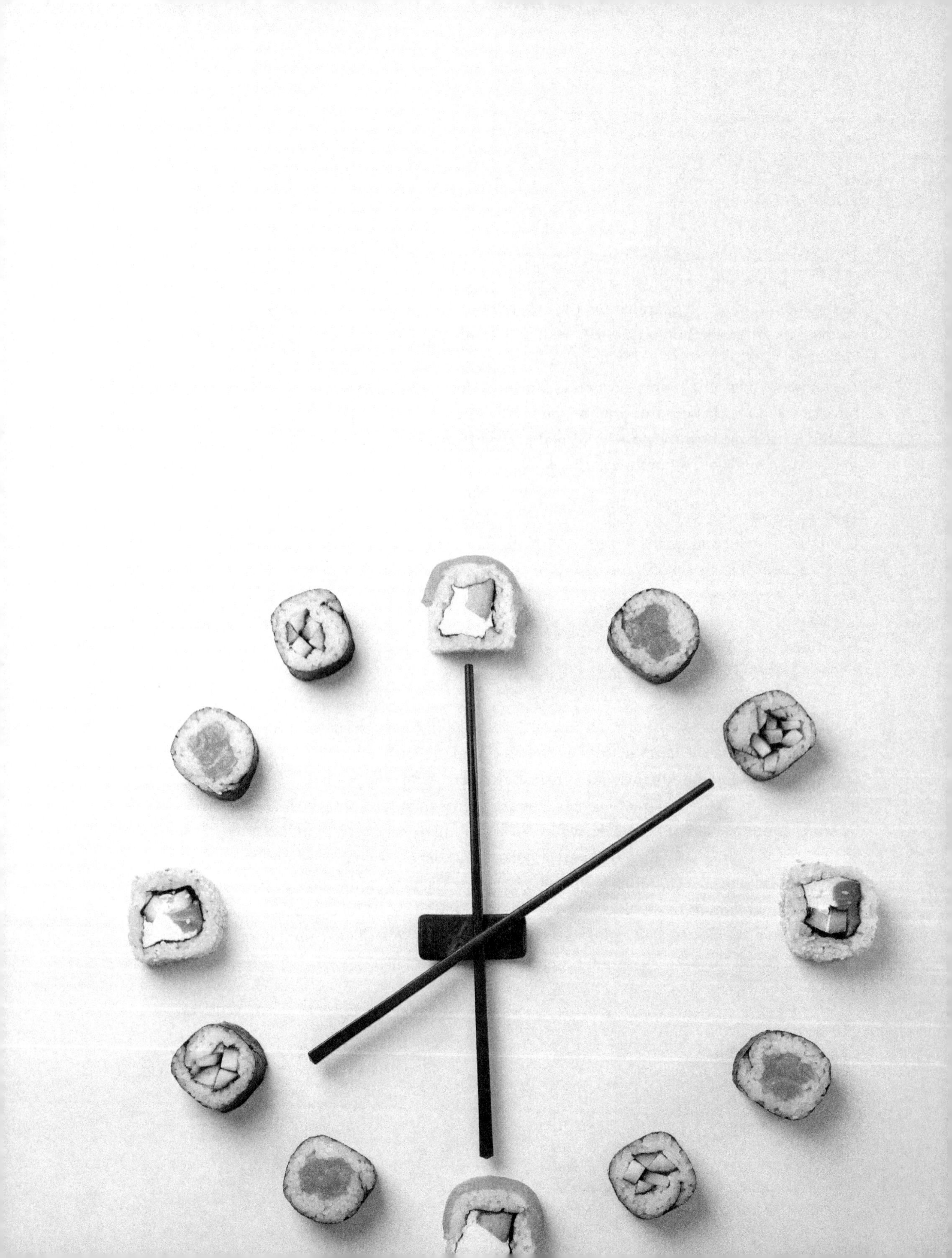

In Japan, sushi has a special place in people's hearts. It's not just a mainstay of Japanese culture, but it's also become a mainstay of contemporary culinary fare.

New tuna factories have been built on a large scale. Onboard the ship, tuna may be prepared for consumption. As a result, these vessels can travel greater distances than any other kind of fishing boat in history. In addition to fulfilling the rising demand for fish, these modern fishing boats were also able to fish in previously inaccessible seas. Fishing advances have been spurred by a need for tuna/sushi and food delivery and packaging innovations. Indeed, shipping fish over great distances was made possible because of innovations such as packing the stomach containing ice & utilizing insulation in specific crates to keep the fish fresh. This prevented any significant damage to or spoilage of the fish during transportation and storage. The global food sector has benefited greatly from innovations like these, which have made it possible to carry precious and delicate products over vast distances without difficulty. We can say that sushi is greatly responsible for all of the fantastic advancements in the worldwide food transport business.

LET'S MAKE SUSHI

The tradition of sushi in Japan began as a means of preserving fish that had been fermented in rice. The rice was then thrown out, and only the fermented fish would remain to be consumed. Over time, the method of preserving fish in this way evolved, and the rice began to be eaten along with the fish. This early form of sushi was known as "nare-zushi," and it was a staple food in Japan for many centuries.

In the 18th and 19th centuries, a new form of sushi known as "Edo-mae sushi" emerged in the city of Edo, which is now known as Tokyo. This type of sushi was made with freshly caught fish and served immediately, rather than being fermented. The sushi rice was also seasoned with vinegar, sugar, and salt, which helped to enhance the flavor of the fish.

Sushi was originally considered a type of fast food in Japan, and was commonly sold at street stalls and markets. It wasn't until the 20th century that sushi began to gain popularity outside of Japan. and went from being a sort of "street food" to become more associated with fine dining.
Today, sushi is enjoyed all over the world and can be found in many different forms, including rolls, bowls, and hand-pressed sushi.

Sushi is made with a wide range of ingredients, including rice, seafood, vegetables, and eggs. Sushi's ingredients can vary widely. However, some common ingredients found in traditional sushi include:

RAW FISH
This is often the most iconic ingredient in sushi and can include a variety of types of fish, such as tuna, salmon, and red snapper.

RICE
The rice that is most commonly used in Sushi is a type of short-grain rice that is seasoned as for tradition with vinegar, salt, and sugar. These combination makes the base for many types of sushi.

VEGETABLES
Sushi can be filled with a variety of vegetables, including cucumber, avocado, carrot, and radish.

SEAWEED
Thin sheets of seaweed, called nori, are often used to wrap rolls of sushi.types of sushi.

EGGS
Thin omelette strips, called tamagoyaki, are often used as a filling in sushi rolls.

PICKLED GINGER
sliced pink ginger is often served with sushi to cleanse your palate. Chewing on a piece of thinly cut ginger before your next sushi will leave you feeling refreshed.

WASABI
This spicy green condiment is often served with sushi and can be used to add a kick to the dish. It is made from the wasabi plant and has a strong, tangy flavor.

SOY SAUCE
A dipping dark, salty sauce made from fermented soybeans, soy sauce is often used to add flavor to sushi.

These are just a few of the many ingredients that can be used in any sushi variation. Of course the combinations are endless, and in fact sushi today uses even more ingredients than ever. Putting some imagination in sushi recipes, as you'll see, is one of my favorite things do to enjoy the Japanese cuisine superstar in a modern way, without forgetting about tradition.

SUSHI VARIETIES

> The most popular type of sushi is known as "nigiri," which consists of a small ball of sushi rice topped with a slice of fish or other seafood. Other popular types of sushi include "maki," which is sushi rice and fillings wrapped in seaweed, and "temaki," which is a cone-shaped roll of sushi.

There are many types of sushi, including:

NIGIRI: The most popular and simple type of sushi, made with a small ball of sushi rice topped with a slice of raw fish or other seafood.

MAKI: This is a type of sushi made by rolling vinegared rice and other ingredients, such as seafood, vegetables, and egg, in a nori seaweed. Maki is usually cut into small, round pieces.

SASHIMI: Sashimi is a sushi typical delicacy that is made by slicing thinly fresh raw fish and it's served without rice.

CHIRASHI: Typical festive dish of sushi usually eaten in little bowls, it is composed of sushi (vinegared) rice with different ingredients (typically rawfish, egg and vegetables) scattered in the mix. "Scattered", in fact is what "chirashi" means.

TEMAKI: This is a popular type of sushi that consists of mixed seafood and vegetables wrapped in a cone-shaped bit of seaweed.

INARI: This is a very peculiar variation of sushi that uses deep-fried tofu pouches with vinegar rice and other ingredients, completely vegetarian or even with meat variations.

OSHI: This is a type of pressed sushi made by layering ingredients, such as seafood and vegetables, with vinegared rice and pressing them together with a wooden mold.

NAREZUSHI: A type of fermented sushi made by curing raw fish in a mixture of rice and salt for several months. It is typically sliced thin and served with soy sauce for a great taste.

TOOLS FOR PREPARING SUSHI

There are many tools and techniques used in the preparation of sushi. One of the most important tools is the "hangiri," which is a large wooden tub used for mixing and cooling the sushi rice. A "hankotsu" or "deba" knife is used to fillet fish, and a "usuba" knife is used for slicing vegetables. A "makisu," or bamboo rolling mat, is also used to roll maki and temaki. There are a few tools and equipment that are commonly used to prepare sushi:

SUSHI MAT: This is a mat made of bamboo or plastic that is used to roll sushi into the desired shape.

SUSHI KNIFE: A sharp knife called a hankotsu is traditionally used to cut sushi into small bite-sized pieces. It is typically made of stainless steel and has a straight edge.

RICE COOKER: This is a kitchen appliance that is used to cook rice to the proper consistency for sushi. It typically has a measuring cup, a non-stick inner pot, and a keep-warm function.

RICE PADDLE: This is a flat wooden paddle that is used to mix and shape the sushi rice.

FOCUS ON: THE MAKISU

The traditional bamboo mat, or makisu, is an essential tool in the preparation of sushi. This simple yet effective kitchen utensil has been used for centuries in Japan to roll and shape sushi into its iconic cylindrical form.

The makisu is made of thin, interwoven bamboo strips that are held together by cotton string, which makes it light, flexible, and easy to handle. This wooden mat has gone through thousands of years and it's still the perfect tool for shaping sushi.

To use the makisu, a chef will lay out a sheet of seaweed, or nori, on top of the mat and then spread a layer of sushi rice over the nori. The chef will then add various fillings, such as raw fish, vegetables, or tofu, onto the rice. The mat is then used to roll the ingredients into a tight, cylindrical shape, with the help of the chef's fingers.

The makisu has a number of benefits that make it the preferred choice for sushi chefs. Firstly, it allows for precise control and consistency in the size and shape of the sushi rolls. This is especially important in a restaurant setting where presentation is key. Secondly, bamboo is a well-known hygienic material and is very easy to clean, making it suitable for use in a kitchen environment.
Finally, the makisu is environmentally friendly and biodegradable, making it a more sustainable choice than plastic alternatives which are recyclable only under specific conditions.

In conclusion, the traditional bamboo mat is an integral tool in the preparation of sushi. Its versatility, precision, and sustainability make it a valuable asset in any sushi chef's kitchen. Today though finding a traditional bamboo mat can be challenging and expensive.

If you don't have one at hand, don't fret: there are a few modern alternatives to the traditional makisu for preparing sushi:

PLASTIC SUSHI MAT: These mats are similar to the traditional bamboo mats, but are made of plastic instead. They are easier to clean and more durable than bamboo mats, but may not be as environmentally friendly.

SUSHI ROLLER: This is a plastic kitchen gadget that is used to roll sushi. It consists of a cylindrical tube with a handle on one end and a flat rolling surface on the other. It is easy to use and allows for precise control of the size and shape of the sushi rolls.

SUSHI PRESS: This is a plastic kitchen gadget that is used to shape sushi into a rectangular or square shape. It consists of two hinged plates that can be clamped together to form a box. The chef places the ingredients on one plate, closes the press, and then removes the finished sushi from the other plate.

SUSHI ROLLING KIT: These kits usually include a plastic mat, a rolling guide, and a cutting tool. They are designed to make the process of rolling sushi easier and more efficient, especially for beginners.

Another cheap alternative is to use a clean kitchen towel or cloth, which in extreme condition will do. So yes, there are many modern alternatives to the traditional makisu for preparing sushi. These tools offer convenience and efficiency, but may not have the same level of precision and authenticity as a traditional bamboo mat.

SUSHI RICE PREPARATION

To prepare rice for sushi, follow these simple steps:

1. Rinse 1 cup of short grain sushi rice under cold water until the water runs clear. By doing this you are separating starch in excess and dirt from the rice.

2. Place the rinsed rice in a saucepan with 1 1/4 cups of water. Bring the water to a boil over high heat.

3. Turn the heat down low and put a tight-fitting lid on the pan. Add rice to boiling water and simmer for 18-20 minutes until all of the water is absorbed.

4. Remove and allow the saucepan to sit for 10 minutes. This will allow the rice to simmer and finish cooking.

5. While the rice is cooking, mix together a sushi vinegar solution by combining 1/4 cup rice vinegar, 2 tablespoons sugar, and 1 teaspoon salt in a small saucepan. Bring the vinegar mixture to a low boil until the salt and sugar have dissolved.

6. When done, pour it into a bowl made from either wood or ceramic. Pour the vinegar mixture over the rice and use a spatula or wooden spoon to gently fold everything together.

7. Fan the rice while you fold it to help it cool and to ensure that the vinegar mixture is evenly distributed. When the rice has cooled to room temperature, it is ready to be used for all kinds of sushi. Enjoy!

RAW FISH PREPARATION

To prepare raw fish for making sushi, you will need to follow these steps:

1. Start by choosing the freshest fish possible. Look for shiny, moist flesh that is free of any discoloration or odd odors.

2. Once you have selected your fish, you will need to clean and fillet it. Rinse the fish under cold running water first to remove any dirt or debris.

3. Next, use a sharp knife to cut off the head, tail, and fins. Then, make a cut along the belly of the fish to remove the entrails.

4. You will now need to remove the skin from the fillets. Make a superficial cut along the length of the fillet, starting at the tail end. Then, use the knife to carefully separate the skin from the flesh, pulling the skin away from the fillet as you go.

5. Once you have removed the skin, use the knife to slice the fillet into thin strips. The strips should be about 1/4 inch thick and 3-4 inches long.

6. Finally, have the sliced fish rest in a bowl of ice water for about 30 minutes to an hour to firm it up and enhance its texture (this is for "tempering" the fish and helps to improve the overall quality of the sushi). Once the fish has been tempered, it is ready to be used in your sushi recipes. Enjoy!

THE PERFECT SUSHI ROLL

The most popular, and loved, kind of sushi is probably the maki, or sushi roll. When you prepare homemade sushi, this is the most satisfying type to surveyor guest, as you can surprise them with the many flavor and fragrance you can customize your rolls with. Here is a step-by-step guide on how to make perfect sushi rolls:

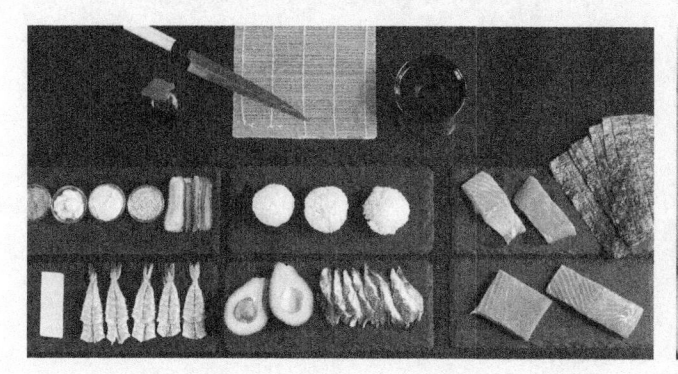

1– Gather all of your ingredients. This usually includes the sushi rice, the fillings of your choice (such as raw fish, vegetables, etc.), nori sheets, and any additional toppings you want to include (such as sesame seeds or roe). Make sure to have everything prepared and within reach before you begin rolling the sushi.

2– Prepare the sushi rice according to your recipe. This usually involves rinsing the rice until the water runs clear, then cooking it with a specific ratio of water to rice. Once the rice is cooked, mix in a seasoned vinegar mixture while the rice is still hot. The rice should be sticky and slightly shiny when it is done.

3– Lay out a makisu or sheet of plastic wrap on your work surface, and place a sheet of nori on top of it. The plastic wrap will help you shape the sushi and keep the rolling process neat and tidy.

4– Lay a thin layer of rice over the nori and spread it leaving a 1-inch border around the edges. The rice should cover the nori evenly, but not be too thick. You can add sesame seed at this point.

5- Place your fillings in a line down the center of the rice. You can use the pletora of fillings you can find in the recipes that follow, such as raw fish, cooked shrimp, vegetables, or tofu ,and more. Be sure to slice the fillings into thin, even strips so that they roll easily.

6 - Raise the edge of the plastic wrap closest to you, and use it to help you roll the sushi away from you into a tight cylinder. The plastic wrap will help shape the sushi as you roll it. Use a little water to wet the border of the nori to help seal the roll. This way the roll will stay together so that no fillings spill out.

7- Cut the roll into slices with a sharp knife. You can wet the blade with a little water to help it slice through the roll more easily. Try to make slices that are 1 to 2 inch thick.

8- Serve the sushi immediately. If desired, accompany it with a little plate with some soy sauce for dipping. Enjoy your homemade sushi!

FOCUS ON: CHOPSTICKS!

Chopsticks have been used as eating utensils in East Asia for thousands of years. It is believed that they were first used in ancient China, and they have been a common utensil in Japan, Korea, and other parts of Asia for centuries. Sushi, which is a type of food that originated in Japan, is traditionally eaten with chopsticks. In Japan, chopsticks are called "hashi" and are made from a variety of materials, including wood, bamboo, and plastic. They are typically about 9 inches long and are held in the dominant hand, with the upper chopstick resting on the thumb and the lower chopstick held between the index finger and middle finger.

Chopsticks are used to pick up individual pieces of sushi and bring them to the mouth. It is considered polite to use chopsticks to eat sushi, and there are certain customs and etiquette that are followed when using chopsticks in Japan. For example, it is considered rude to stick your chopsticks upright into a bowl of rice, as this is reminiscent of the way rice is offered to the dead in Japanese funerary rituals. It is also considered bad manners to wave your chopsticks around or to use them to point at people or objects.

If you visit Japan you will realize that in most venues it is perfectly fine to eat sushi with bare hands. It really depends on the context and the restaurant, a good indication is to take a look at the chef, how does she cook and how the food is offered to you. Some high end restaurants value so much the craft of making sushi and the connection with it that it is not unusual to have nigiri offered to you from the chef's palm! In these places it is expected that customers will eat with their hands, and they are even given a special towel to clean hands between items. Only do not take sashimi with you hands, that's never ok.

SUSHI SAUCES

While sushi is often enjoyed on its own, there are a variety of sauces that can be used to add flavor and depth to the dish.
One of the most popular sauces used with sushi is SOY SAUCE, which is made from soybeans, salt, wheat, and fermented. Soy sauce has a rich, salty flavor that pairs well with the delicate flavors of raw fish and other ingredients used in sushi. It is typically served as a dipping sauce and can be used to enhance the flavor of the sushi as well as to add a touch of moisture to the dish.

Another sauce commonly used with sushi is WASABI, a spicy green condiment derived by the root of a plant called Wasabia japonica. Wasabi's fiery flavor is often used as a condiment for sushi and sashimi. It is typically served as a small dab on the side of the plate and is used to add a burst of heat to the dish.

Other sauces that are commonly used with sushi include PONZU sauce, a citrus-based sauce made from soy sauce, vinegar, and citrus juice; and EEL sauce, a sweet and savory sauce made from soy sauce and mirin that is commonly used as a topping for eel sushi. In addition to these traditional sauces, there are also many modern variations that are used to add flavor to sushi.

Some examples include SPICY MAYO, a mixture of mayonnaise and sriracha sauce; and HONEY MUSTARD sauce, a combination of mustard and honey that is often used as a topping for sushi rolls.

As you can see, there are many different sauces that can be used to enhance the flavor of sushi. Whether you prefer the classic taste of soy sauce and wasabi or the more modern twist of spicy mayo and honey mustard, there is a sauce out there to suit every taste. I'm going to share with you my recipes for two of my favorite sauces, one classic, the TERIYAKI and another for more exotic tastes, the SPICY MANGO SAUCE, a favorite of mine.

SPICY MANGO SAUCE

Spicy mango sauce is a flavorful and slightly sweet condiment that can be used to add a tropical twist to sushi and other dishes. Here is a simple recipe for making spicy mango sauce at home.

INGREDIENTS

- 1 ripe mango, peeled and diced
- 2 tablespoons rice vinegar
- 1 small jalapeno pepper, seeded and diced
- 1 tablespoon water
- 1 tablespoon sugar
- 1/2 teaspoon red pepper flakes (optional)
- 1/2 teaspoon salt

INSTRUCTIONS

1. In a small saucepan, combine the soy sauce, sake or mirin, and sugar. Add the minced garlic and grated ginger

2. Place the saucepan over medium heat and bring the mixture to a boil. Reduce the heat to low and simmer for 5-10 minutes, or until the sauce has thickened and reduced by about one-third.

3. Remove the mixture from the heat. Let it cool to room temperature. You can use the space right away or store it in an airtight container in the refrigerator for up to one week.

TERIYAKI SAUCE

Teriyaki sauce is a popular condiment in Japanese cuisine that is used to add flavor to a variety of dishes, including sushi.

The word "teriyaki" actually refers to a technique to cook food, specifically when the food is grilled (or broiled) and coated with a sweet yet salty glaze. The sauce itself is made from a combination of soy sauce, sake (a Japanese rice wine), mirin (a sweet rice wine), and sugar. There are many variations of teriyaki sauce, with some versions being sweeter, saltier, or thicker than others. The traditional method for making teriyaki sauce involves simmering the ingredients together until the sugar has dissolved and the sauce has condensed.

Some modern variations may include additional ingredients such as garlic, ginger, or other spices to give the sauce a more elaborate flavor. Teriyaki sauce is often used as a marinade for meats such as chicken, beef, and pork, but it can also be used as a dipping sauce or topping for dishes like sushi and sashimi. The sweet and savory flavor of the sauce pairs well with the delicate flavors of raw fish, and it can help to balance out the taste of some of the more pungent ingredients used in sushi, such as wasabi or pickled ginger. If being delicious wasn't enough, teriyaki sauce is also healthy.

Indeed, soy sauce, one of its main ingredients, is a good source of antioxidants and has anti-inflammatory properties. Moreover, a byproduct of the fermentation process used to make soy sauce are probiotics, which can help to improve gut health.

Overall, teriyaki sauce is a delicious and versatile condiment that adds flavor and depth to a wide range of dishes, including sushi. Whether you are using it as a marinade, a dipping sauce, or a topping, teriyaki sauce is sure to add an extra layer of flavor to your meal.

INGREDIENTS

- 1/2 cup soy sauce
- 1/2 cup sake (Japanese rice wine) or mirin
- 1/2 cup sugar
- 2 cloves garlic, minced
- 1-inch piece ginger, grated

INSTRUCTIONS

1. In a small saucepan, combine the soy sauce, sake or mirin, and sugar. Add the minced garlic and grated ginger

2. Place the saucepan over medium heat and bring the mixture to a boil. Reduce the heat to low and simmer for 5-10 minutes, or until the sauce has thickened and reduced by about one-third.

3. Remove the mixture from the heat. Let it cool to room temperature.

4. You can use the space right away or store it in an airtight container in the refrigerator for up to one week.

LET'S JUMP INTO THE R CI

E

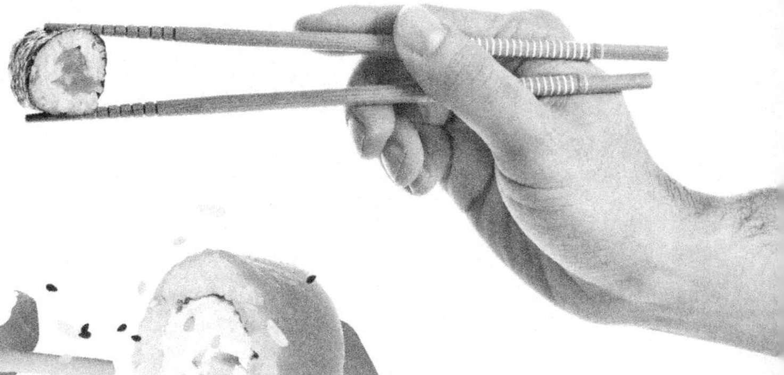

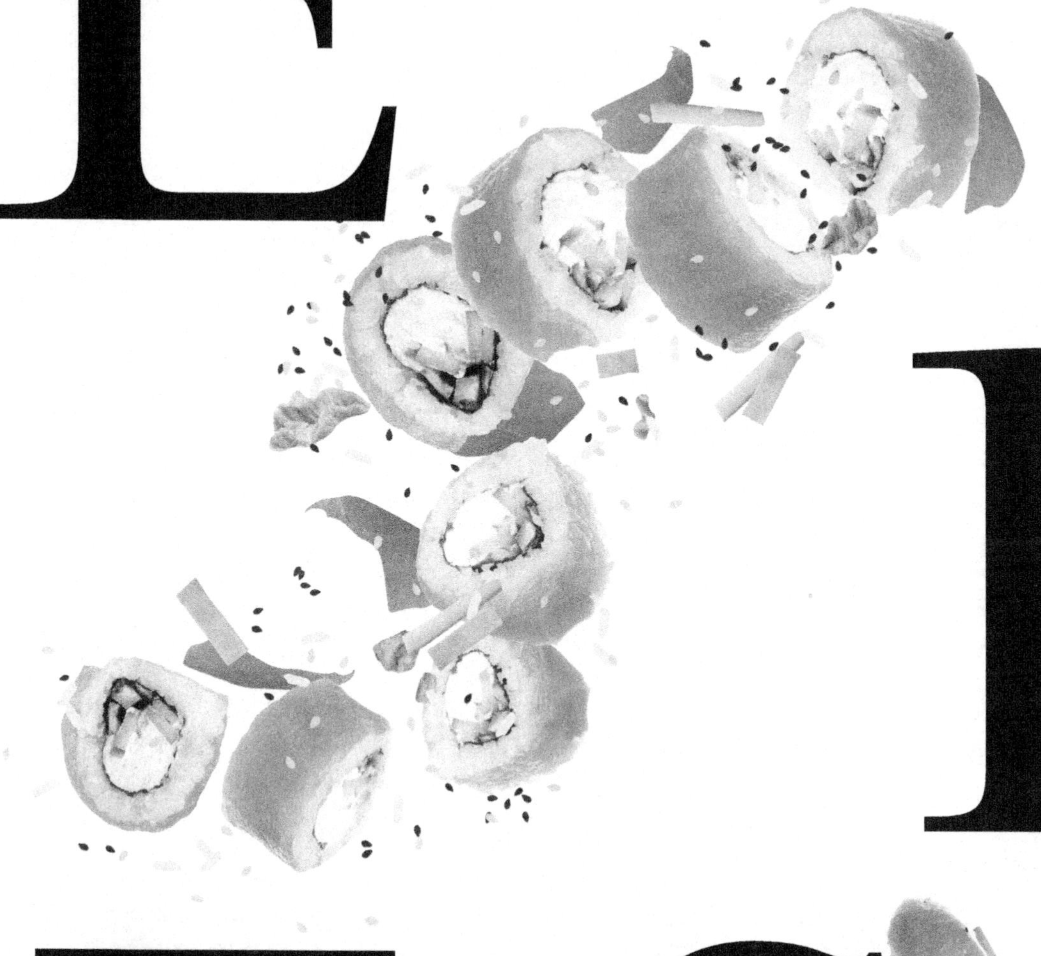

P

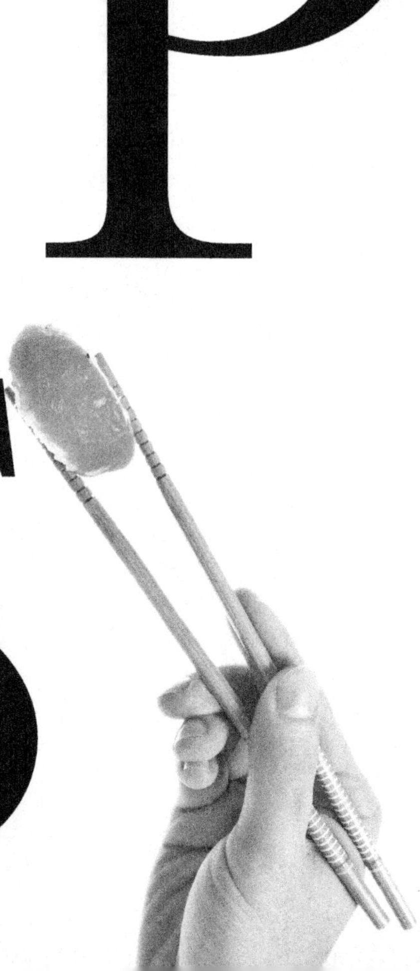

E S

MAKI AND NIGIRI SUSHI

Prep Time — **30 MIN**
Cooking Time — **40 MIN**
Servings — **4**

INGREDIENTS

Rice
- 1 & ½ cups grain sushi rice
- 1 & ½ cups water cold

Zu
- ½ cup vinegar rice
- 2 teaspoons salt kosher
- 2 tablespoons sugar

Sushi
- 1-1 & ¼ pounds grade fish sashimi
- 4-5 Nori sheets

NUTRITION

Calories 354 Kcal
Carbs 11 g | Fat 21 g
Protein 35 g

INSTRUCTIONS

MAKE RICE & ZU

1. Prepare the dry sushi rice by weighing or measuring 1-2 cups and rinsing it approximately three times, or unless all water is clear. Mix rice with your hands by adding ice water to a bowl and stirring. Then drain the rice and repeat this procedure. Place the rice in a saucepan, add 1-2 cups of cold water, and let your rice soak for around 15 minutes.

2. Bring water and rice to a boil over medium-high heat in a medium saucepan. Cover closely with a lid when bubbles develop around the pot's edge and reduce heat to a very low setting. A timer for ten minutes has been set up.

3. Meanwhile, prepare the zu. A small dish of rice vinegar mixed with salt and sugar should have the salt and sugar dissolved. Put the zu in the fridge.

4. After ten minutes, turn off the heat and keep the lid closed. 9 minutes later, please remove it from the fridge. Take the cover off after 9 minutes and taste the rice. Tender & sticky with just a touch of chew, it should be. Gently pour the rice out from a wet hangiri or a big dry glass/pyrex bowl using the wooden rice spoon.

5. Then, while the rice is hot, use a "dry paddle" to spread your zu over it. While swinging back & forth on the rice in the sideways chopping movement with the paddle, gently pour your zu on the paddle. The zu will be spread out equally, and the rice will be cooled simultaneously.

Once all your zu has been poured into the bowl, use the paddle to chop and fling the rice in a sideways motion. Don't mash the potatoes. The idea is to spread your rice, scatter the Zu and chill the rice simultaneously. Spread and cut the rice a second time in the middle of the pyrex bowl. Gently gather the rice after it has been distributed twice and press it with a moist cotton cloth. Replenish rice in a bowl, flip over, and discard the towel. A moist towel may be used to protect rice without drying. Set the rice aside for now. Neither in the freezer nor on the countertop.

MAKING THE MAKI

6. If feasible, cut the fish into strips that are 1/8- to 1/4-inch broad and as long as the nori sheet. Set the fish aside.

7. Dip your hands in a water bowl before washing them. Place one nori sheet on the bottom of the rolling bamboo mat. Using your palm, take a "cue ball"-sized portion of rice and lay it in the middle of a nori sheet. Dip your hands into the water to gently cover them. Use the fingers to distribute the rice evenly over the surface, covering all the edges and corners. The top nori sheet should be left without rice by approximately ¼ inch. When you're ready to roll the nori, add a few rice grains to the part that doesn't have any.

8. Sprinkle sesame seeds on the nori sheet after the rice has been carefully distributed throughout the nori sheet. Slice a piece of fish over the whole width of the sheet. Cucumber, avocado, other favorite ingredients, or even extra fish may be added. It would be best if you didn't overstuff the roll; in this case, less really is more.

9. As you lift the edges of a bamboo mat, keep the fish and vegetables in place and roll your mat and nori sheet over & onto itself in a cylinder form. Tighten & secure your fish and accessories by gently pulling the mat and nori sheet along the roll length. When the nori sheet is fully rolled over, the rice at the top should be glued to the back of a nori sheet. Make a seal by gently squeezing and sliding the hand across the whole mat with a roll inside. Finally, unroll your mat and place it seam-side down on a flat surface. This will assist in strengthening the seal.

26 FISH

10. Make separate bite-sized makis by slicing through the roll with a thin-bladed knife that has been wetted with water. Soy sauce or wasabi may be slathered over the maki or both. Cleanse the palate with sake or ginger if necessary.

MAKE NIGIRI

11. Cut the fish into 1-1 1/2-inch broad and 2-inch-long pieces, then place them in a baking dish. Slice with grain if you're using fatty fish like king salmon or sablefish. Slice most other fish against the grain to make it more delicate. Refrigerate the fish slices to keep them fresh.

MAKE SUSHI RICE

12. Wet your hands and remove the fish from the refrigerator. Gently hold one and a half tablespoons of rice in your palm like a baby bird. Place the rice into your cupped palm and softly but firmly push down with your index & middle fingers on top of it with your opposite hand. As you curl your fingers together, hold for three seconds. Once again, gently spin the rice "cushion" by lifting your fingers and holding it for three seconds as you push your fingers into it.

13. Wasabi should be sparingly placed on the rice "pillow," which you are still holding. Then, top the rice with a piece of fish. Using the same two fingers, gently yet firmly push the fish & rice together.

EASY SALMON SUSHI RICE BOWL

- Prep Time — **10 MIN**
- Cooking Time — **20 MIN**
- Servings — **2**

INGREDIENTS

- 150 g rice sushi
- caster sugar pinch
- 1 tbsp vinegar rice
- 120 g edamame frozen
- 1 carrot large
- radishes handful
- ¼ cucumber
- 2 salmon fillets cooked skinless
- 1 to 2 tbsp sauce soy
- 1 tsp sesame seeds toasted
- sushi ginger few pieces

INSTRUCTIONS

1. Toss the sushi rice with a touch of salt in a medium pot with 200ml water. Take a pan and put the heat up to medium. Cook for 15 minutes on low heat with a lid on the pan once it has reached boiling point.

2. After 15 minutes, remove the pan from the heat, fluff the rice with a fork, and cover it again; the rice will cook for another 5 minutes. After 5 minutes, check the rice for doneness — it should be soft but not mushy, and the water should have been absorbed. Recover with the lid and let too warm as you prep the remaining ingredients and stir in the sugar and vinegar.

3. Bring a small saucepan of water to a medium boil on the stovetop. Add your edamame beans and simmer for 3 minutes, then drain well.

4. Using a vegetable peeler, remove the outer layer of carrot skin and continue peeling until you have a thick ribbon of carrot flesh.

5. Slice the radishes into quarters. Using a mandolin, shave the cucumber into long, thin slices.

6. With the hands, break up the fish into little pieces, eyeing for other bone fragments.

7. Stack the sushi rice and other ingredients in two bowls, then sprinkle with soy sauce & sesame seeds, if desired, before serving.

NUTRITION

Calories 725 Kcal
Carbs 73 g | Fat 27 g
Protein 41 g

KANPACHI NIGIRI

Prep Time — **60 MIN**
Cooking Time — **30 MIN**
Servings — **4**

INGREDIENTS

- 3.5 oz of fresh amberjack fillet
- 7 oz of sushi rice (prepared and seasoned with sushi vinegar)
- Wasabi paste
- Soy sauce (for dipping)
- Pickled ginger (for cleansing the palate)

INSTRUCTIONS

1. Prepare the Amberjack: Start with a high-quality, sushi-grade amberjack fillet. With a sharp knife, slice the amberjack into thin pieces, about 5mm thick, ensuring each slice is uniform to achieve a harmonious balance in every nigiri.

2. Shape the Sushi Rice: Wet your hands with water mixed with a bit of rice vinegar to prevent sticking. Take about 20 grams (0.7 oz) of sushi rice and gently form it into a small, oblong mound. Be sure not to compress the rice too firmly; it should be lightly packed so that it falls apart in your mouth, offering a contrast to the fish's texture.

3. Assemble the Nigiri: Place a small dab of wasabi on the rice mound, then lay a slice of amberjack over it. Gently press the fish onto the rice to ensure they bond without squashing the rice. The wasabi adds a subtle heat that complements the amberjack's natural flavors.

4. Serving: Serve the nigiri on a minimalist plate, accompanied by soy sauce for dipping and pickled ginger. The simplicity of the presentation highlights the beauty and taste of the amberjack.

NUTRITION

Calories 300 Kcal
Protein 20g
Carbohydrates 40g | Fat 5g

NIGIRI SPECIAL / SEAFOOD MEDLEY

Prep Time — **10 MIN**
Cooking Time — **25 MIN**
Servings — **4**

INGREDIENTS

- 320 g rice sushi
- 80 ml vinegar sushi
- seaweed nori
- sushi mold nigiri
- paste wasabi
- sauce soy
- ginger ideas for pickled sushi
- raw fish fresh, yellowtail or tuna
- salmon smoked
- prawns cooked
- squid or cooked octopus
- eel grilled
- sticks crab
- style omelet tamagoyaki Japanese
- avocado
- mushrooms shiitake

NUTRITION

Calories 224 Kcal
Carbs 17 g | Fat 8 g
Protein 30 g

INSTRUCTIONS

1. To begin making nigiri sushi, you must first prepare the sushi rice. Follow our recipe in chaper one.

2. The microwaveable rice will save you time and effort while preparing a meal. To make sushi rice vinegar, combine 250 g of cooked rice with 1 tbsp of rice sushi vinegar.

3. While your rice is simmering, preparation of the fish, veggies, or other desired toppings may be done. Tamagoyaki, a tasty Japanese-style omelet, is also a favorite sushi garnish. Tofu, pickles, sun-dried tomatoes, avocado, and smoked salmon are good alternatives to raw fish. The length of a slice doesn't need to be exact; just make it large enough to cover most of the rice pod & thick enough to obtain the entire flavor.

4. Finally, the rice pods are ready! Sushi experts use a mixture of water & sushi vinegar to keep their hands clean and prevent the rice from sticking. Using the nigiri sushi mold is a simple approach to consistently producing beautiful rice pods. Make sure that the rice is distributed properly, and then push the lid down and turn it back over so that you can get all of it.

5. Adding a little wasabi to the bottom of your topping will give it that extra kick. Finally, press your topping onto the sushi rice pod tightly while keeping your arms wet with water & vinegar. A strip of nori seaweed keeps the rice pod's cap from sliding off when making tamagoyaki.

CALIFORNIA ROLL SUSHI

- Prep Time — **45 MIN**
- Cooking Time — **45 MIN**
- Servings — **8 ROLLS**

INGREDIENTS

- 1 cup of uncooked white rice short grain
- 1 cup of water
- ¼ cup vinegar rice
- 1 tbsp sugar white
- ½ cup finely chopped crabmeat
- ¼ cup of mayonnaise
- 8 dry seaweed nori sheets
- 2 & ½ tbsp seeds sesame
- 1 cut in thin spears cucumber
- 2 pitted, peeled, & sliced long way avocados

NUTRITION

Calories 232 Kcal
Carbs 23.7 g | Fat 14 g
Protein 4 g

INSTRUCTIONS

1. Using several water changes, rinse and drain the rice, then put in the rice cooker or covered pan with water & let it simmer for about 1 hr. Heat till boiling, then decrease the heat to keep the gentle mixture simmering. Allow your rice to cook for approximately 15 mins or until the top is dry. Turn the heat down & leave for around 10 mins to allow the remaining water to be absorbed by the pasta.

2. Combine rice vinegar, sugar, & salt in a separate bowl stir into your cooked rice unless well incorporated. Set the rice aside to cool down.

3. Set aside the mayonnaise & crabmeat in a dish. The bamboo rolling pad should be covered using plastic wrap before rolling sushi. Place a nori sheet on the plastic wrap, shiny side up. Apply a thin, uniform layer of cooked rice to the nori using damp fingertips, leaving ¼ inch of the sheet exposed at the bottom border. Add half sesame seeds & gently push them into the rice until they're evenly distributed. The seaweed side of the nori sheet should face up.

4. All along with a nori sheet, around a quarter of the way from the exposed side, arrange 2-3 medium cucumber spears, 2-3 pieces of avocado, & approximately 1 tbsp of imitation crab mix. Tightly roll your sushi until it is approximately 1 ½ inch in diameter, then cut it in half to remove any excess filling from the sushi. It is necessary to carefully compress tightly compacted sushi once the roll is wrapped in a mat.

5. Use a sharp knife soaked in water to cut every roll into 1" pieces.

CRAB AND AVOCADO SUSHI

Prep Time — **60 MIN**
Cooking Time — **10 MIN**
Servings — **8**

INGREDIENTS

- 1 Japanese cucumber
- 1 teaspoon wasabi
- 8 nigiri rice balls Sixteen 2-in (5-cm)-long crab pieces
- Eight 2-in (5-cm)-long avocado slices
- Soy sauce for dipping

INSTRUCTIONS

1. Using a vegetable peeler, slice 8 long ribbons from the cucumber.
2. Prepare the nigiri rice balls. Top each nigiri rice ball with 1/8 teaspoon of wasabi, a slice of avocado and two pieces of crab.
3. Use a cucumber ribbon as a "belt" to wrap around each piece of sushi to help hold the ingredients together.

NUTRITION

Calories 444 Kcal
Carbs 80 g | Fat 8 g | Protein 10 g

CRAB STICK SALAD CANAPÉ

Prep Time — **15 MIN**
Cooking Time — **10 MIN**
Servings — **4 ROLLS**

INGREDIENTS

- 2 surimi sticks or 1 oz (30 g) freshly cooked crab meat
- 1 tablespoon mayonnaise
- 1/8 teaspoon soy sauce
- 7 or 8 kaiware daikon sprouts or broccoli sprouts, chopped
- 4 rice-half filled canapé cups

INSTRUCTIONS

1. Cook the rice and divide it evenly in the 4 cups and shred the crab sticks or crab meat into small pieces.
2. Combining the mayonnaise and soy sauce with the crab meat and mix well. To obtain a crab salad.
3. Mix in the sprouts, and place 1/4 of the salad on each of the 4 rice-filled cups.

NUTRITION

Calories 444 Kcal
Carbs 80 g | Fat 8 g | Protein 10 g

FISH

SIMPLE SMOKED SALMON SUSHI

Prep Time — **60 MIN**
Cooking Time — **10 MIN**
Servings — **8**

INGREDIENTS

- 1 standard quantity of Simple White Rice
- 2 tablespoons lemon juice
- 2 tablespoons capers
- 1 1/2 tablespoons sugar
- 3 tablespoons rice vinegar
- 1/2 teaspoon salt
- 6 slices of smoked salmon (about 4 1/2 oz/125 g total)
- Few sprigs of fresh dill for garnish
- Few slices of lemon for garnish

INSTRUCTIONS

1. Prepare the Simple White Rice. Add the lemon juice and capers, and mix gently but well.

2. Combine the sugar, rice vinegar and salt in a small bowl and mix well to make a marinade. Soak the smoked salmon slices in the marinade for about 5 minutes.

3. Use a sheet of plastic wrap to line a narrow container, such as a 3 1/2 by 7 inch (9 by 18 cm) mini pound cake pan that's about 2 1/2 inches (6.25 cm) deep. Use enough plastic wrap so that 4 to 5 inches (10 to 12 cm) extends beyond either side of the container. Arrange the salmon slices, so they completely cover the bottom of the container, cutting them to fit if necessary. Cover the salmon with the rice.

4. Fold the edges of the plastic wrap over the rice and press down firmly to form the sushi into a "cake."

5. Turn the sushi out onto a serving dish and remove the plastic wrap. Cut it into pieces and garnish with dill and lemon slices.

NUTRITION

Calories 234 Kcal
Carbs 51 g | Fat 0.3 g
Protein 4 g

NEW YORK ROLL / SHRIMP, AVOCADO, CUCUMBER ROLL

Prep Time — **30 MIN**
Cooking Time — **20 MIN**
Servings — **4**

INGREDIENTS

For your sushi rice

- 3 cups Japanese rice cooked
- 40 ml vinegar Rice
- 1 tbsp of Sugar
- ¾ tsp of Salt

For rolls

- 6 oz shrimp Cooked
- 1 diced Cucumber
- 1 large Avocado
- 3 sheets Nori dried seaweed
- seeds Sesame

INSTRUCTIONS

1. Add rice vinegar, sugar, & salt to a container of cooked rice. Combine thoroughly.
2. Put a bamboo mat in a water bowl with rice vinegar & serve with plastic wrap on the side.
3. Lay 1 nori sheet on bamboo mat with glossy side down. When the nori sheet is wet w/ vinegar water, add rice to middle of nori sheet.
4. Evenly distribute the rice over the nori sheet in a single layer using the fingers. Spread half a tsp of sesame seeds equally over the rice.
5. Rice should face down on the nori sheet. Ensure the nori sheet doesn't go too near the bamboo mat's bottom.
6. Place the cucumber, shrimp, & avocado just on nori horizontally. Each component should be arranged in a cross-hatched pattern.
7. Hold onto the bottom borders of the mat using your thumbs while using your other fingers to grasp the toppings in place.
8. Lift the bamboo mat's edges to keep this from rolling in the roll with the filling. Roll tightly. Your mat should resemble a C from the side as you roll forward. Use some pressure to keep rolling forward, but release when the roll is complete.
9. Take half of the roll and divide it into thirds. Serve with some wasabi & soy sauce.

NUTRITION

Calories 520 g
Carbs 68 g | Fat 14 g
Protein 10 g

34 FISH

TUNA DELIGHT NIGIRI

Prep Time — **60 MIN**
Cooking Time — **35 MIN**
Servings — **4**

INGREDIENTS

- 4 cups of water
- 2 cups white rice uncooked
- ½ cup rice vinegar seasoned
- 1 tsp sugar white
- 1 tsp of salt
- ¼ lb yellowtail hamachi
- ¼ lb tuna maguro
- ¼ lb of cooked shelled & butterflied Ebi shrimp
- 6 large eggs
- ½ tsp sugar white
- ☒ tsp of salt
- 1 tsp Optional wasabi paste
- 1 cut into 1" strips sheet nori

INSTRUCTIONS

1. In a saucepan, bring the water & rice to a boil on high heat. Simmer for 20-25 mins, with the heat reduced to medium-low and the lid on, until your rice is cooked and liquid is absorbed. Use a wooden spoon or rice paddle to transfer the rice to the bowl and mix in the rice vinegar. Season with one tsp of sugar and one tsp of salt, or to your liking. Allow 30 mins for the mixture to settle to ambient temperature.

2. Set aside 2" long and 1" broad fish strips for wrapping. Slice against the grain. Refrigerate until you're ready to eat it!

3. Using a fork, combine the eggs with the sugar and salt in a small bowl until well combined. Over medium heat, cook a thin layer of a quarter of the mix in a large, oiled pan. Cook for around 2 to 3 mins without stirring. Make a log and place it on the pan on one side. You may make a single huge log by re-rolling one-quarter of the egg mixture. Cut the omelet into ½-inch-thick slices by cutting it against the grain.

4. You may apply a little wasabi paste to a slice of shrimp or fish. Assemble a little nugget with one to two tbsp of rice by rolling it in your fingers. The rice ball should be placed over shrimp or fish and squeezed lightly to stick. Assemble the rest of the fish and shrimp while this is done.

5. Take a piece of egg omelet, take 1-2 tbsp of rice, & form it into a little nugget in your palm. Squeeze the rice ball carefully to adhere to the egg before placing it on top.

6. To seal every box, wet one edge of a nori strip & press it into the packet.

NUTRITION

Calories 555 Kcal
Carbs 76 g | Fat 10 g
Protein 35 g

BROWN RICE SMOKED SALMON ROLLS

- Prep Time — **60 MIN**
- Cooking Time — **30 MIN**
- Servings — **2**

INGREDIENTS

- 1 standard quantity of Brown Sushi Rice
- 10 sprigs of fresh dill, chopped
- 10 baby gherkins 1 sheet nori, cut in half
- 12 slices of smoked salmon (about 10 oz/300 g total)
- Wasabi

INSTRUCTIONS

1. Prepare the Brown Sushi Rice.

2. Mix the dill into the Brown Sushi Rice. Divide the rice into two large portions.

3. Place half a sheet of nori on a bamboo mat. Take 1/3 of one large rice portion and spread it evenly over the nori, leaving about 1 inch (2.5 cm) of nori exposed along the edge farthest away from you—this will be the last edge of the nori to be rolled up.

4. Line up 1/2 of the baby gherkins end to end along the center of the rice. Roll up the pickles inside the rice to make a narrow roll. Set this aside.

5. Place a sheet of plastic wrap over the bamboo mat and spread the remaining Brown Sushi Rice on it in a rectangular shape as wide as the length of the narrow roll. Place the narrow roll on top of this rice and roll it up into a thicker roll with the Brown Sushi Rice on the outside.

6. On a fresh piece of plastic wrap on the mat, lay out the salmon slices in a row that is the length of the thick roll. The slices should be overlapping and placed at about a 30-degree angle. Dab them lightly with wasabi.

7. Unwrap the thick roll and place it on top of the salmon slices. Roll it up in the bamboo mat to give the salmon roll its shape.

8. Remove the roll from the bamboo mat and plastic wrap, and place it on a cutting board

NUTRITION

Calories 291 Kcal
Carbs 51 g | Fat 5 g
Protein 10 g

with the salmon side up. Drape it with the plastic wrap again, followed by the bamboo mat. Apply gentle pressure to the bamboo mat along the bottom of the roll so that the mat pulls the salmon firmly down onto the rice roll and gives the top of the roll a smooth, uniform surface.

9. Move the mat so that one edge is even with one end of the roll, and tuck in any loose or uneven rice to give the roll a neat appearance. Repeat for the other end of the roll.

10. Remove the bamboo mat and slice the roll while it is still covered in plastic, using a very sharp knife that you have dampened by wiping it with a moist cloth. Then remove the wrap.

11. Use the remaining ingredients to repeat the process to make a second roll.

MARINATED TUNA HAND ROLLS

Prep Time — **60 MIN**
Cooking Time — **10 MIN**
Servings — **8**

INGREDIENTS

- 1/3 standard quantity Basic Sushi Rice
- 4 1/2 oz (125 g) fresh tuna, cut into 8 sticks
- 4 chives, cut into 4-in (10-cm) lengths
- 4 sheets of nori, cut in half

Yukke Marinade

- 1 tablespoon soy sauce
- 1 teaspoon sesame oil
- ½ teaspoon sugar
- 1 tablespoon white sesame seeds, roasted

INSTRUCTIONS

1. Prepare the Basic Sushi Rice.

2. Mix together all of the ingredients for the Yukke Marinade and marinate the tuna for 5 minutes.

3. Place 1 to 2 tablespoons of sushi rice just to the right of the center of half a sheet of nori. Arrange one piece of tuna and some chives on the rice.

4. Lift the lower right-hand corner of the nori, bring it over the ingredients and tuck it under the middle of the left side of the rice. Then roll the remaining loose nori around the fillings like a cone. Repeat with the remaining ingredients to make 8 rolls.

NUTRITION

Calories 238 Kcal
Carbs 31 g | Fat 2 g
Protein 12 g

SUSHI SPAGHETTI SALAD

- Prep Time — **10 MIN**
- Cooking Time — **10 MIN**
- Servings — **6**

INGREDIENTS

- 375 g spaghetti package
- 8 oz shredded surimi crabmeat
- 1 cup cucumber chopped
- 2 sliced green onions
- ¼ cup oil canola
- 2 tbsp sauce soy
- 2 tbsp vinegar rice wine
- 1 tbsp pickled ginger chopped
- 2 tsp sesame seeds toasted
- 1 tsp oil sesame
- 1 diced ripe avocado
- 1 toasted & torn sheet nori

INSTRUCTIONS

1. Cook the spaghetti as per directions on the box. Transfer to a medium bowl after draining and rinsing with cold water. Toss spaghetti with surimi, cucumber, and green onion.

2. Add soy sauce, ginger, wine vinegar, & sesame seeds to a blender and blend until smooth. Toss the pasta salad with the dressing and evenly distribute the dressing.

3. Transform the dish onto a big serving tray and serve immediately. Before serving, scatter avocado & toasted nori over the top. Move the mat so that one edge is even with one end of the roll, and tuck in any loose or uneven rice to give the roll a neat appearance. Repeat for the other end of the roll.

4. Remove the bamboo mat and slice the roll while it is still covered in plastic, using a very sharp knife that you have dampened by wiping it with a moist cloth. Then remove the wrap.

5. Use the remaining ingredients to repeat the process to make a second roll.

NUTRITION

Calories 426 Kcal
Carbs 52 g | Fat 17 g
Protein 16 g

COCKTAIL SUSHI

- Prep Time — **60 MIN**
- Cooking Time — **30 MIN**
- Servings — **12**

INGREDIENTS

- 1 standard quantity Sushi Rice

Tuna Collins

- 1 1/2 oz (40 g) fresh tuna, cut into small dice
- 1 teaspoon soy sauce
- 1/2 avocado, cut into small pieces
- A few broccoli sprouts or kaiware daikon sprouts for garnish

Egg Nog

- 1 egg
- 1 tablespoon sugar
- Dash of Salt
- 1 teaspoon mirin
- 4 sprigs of chervil or parsley for garnish

Cheese-Mopolitan

- 1/3 Japanese cucumber, finely diced (30 g)
- 1 oz (30 g) tomatoes, finely diced
- 1 oz (30 g) Monterey Jack or other natural cheese, finely diced

INSTRUCTIONS

1. Prepare the Sushi Rice. Divide it into 3 portions.
2. To make the Tuna Collins sushi, marinate the diced tuna in the soy sauce for 5 minutes. Add the tuna and the avocado to one portion of the Basic Sushi Rice. Mix gently and divide the rice among four cocktail glasses (or other serving dishes). Garnish with the sprouts, and cut them into small lengths.
3. To make the Egg Nog sushi, mix the egg, sugar, salt and mirin in a microwave-safe bowl. Microwave for 1 minute and mix well with a fork. Microwave once again for another 30 seconds and mix once again, this time thoroughly with a fork, to make a very fine scrambled egg. Gently mix the egg into the second portion of Basic Sushi Rice and divide it among four cocktail glasses (or other serving dishes). Garnish each with a sprig of chervil or parsley.
4. To make the Cheese-mopolitan sushi, gently mix the diced cucumber, tomatoes and cheese into the third portion of Basic Sushi Rice. Divide the rice among four cocktail glasses (or other serving dishes).

NUTRITION

Calories 238 Kcal
Carbs 31 g | Fat 2 g
Protein 12 g

CRAB STICK SALAD CANAPÉ

Prep Time — **15 MIN**
Cooking Time — **10 MIN**
Servings — **4**

INGREDIENTS

- 2 surimi sticks or 30 g freshly cooked crab meat
- 15 g mayonnaise
- 1/8 teaspoon soy sauce
- 7 or 8 kaiware daikon sprouts or broccoli sprouts, chopped
- 4 rice-half filled canapé cups

INSTRUCTIONS

1. Cook the rice and divide it evenly in the 4 cups. Shred the crab sticks or crab meat into small pieces.
2. Combining the mayonnaise and soy sauce with the crab meat and mix well. To obtain a crab salad.
3. Mix in the sprouts, and place 1/4 of the salad on each of the 4 rice-filled cups.

NUTRITION

Calories 444 Kcal
Carbs 80 g | Fat 8 g | Protein 10 g

SALMON ROE CANAPÉ

Prep Time — **15 MIN**
Cooking Time — **10 MIN**
Servings — **4**

INGREDIENTS

- 2 oz (50 g) fresh salmon roe
- 1/2 teaspoon soy sauce
- 1/2 teaspoon mirin
- 4 rice-filled canapé cups
- 4 fresh shiso leaves

INSTRUCTIONS

1. Marinate the salmon roe in the soy sauce and mirin for at least 30 minutes in your refrigerator.
2. Place each shiso leaf on a portion of rice and top with a spoonful of the marinated salmon roe.

NUTRITION

Calories 356 Kcal
Carbs 43 g | Fat 15 g | Protein 12 g

FISH

CREAM CHEESE & CRAB ROLLS

- Prep Time — **80 MIN**
- Cooking Time — **20 MIN**
- Servings — **2 ROLLS**

INGREDIENTS

- 1 cup white rice uncooked
- 2 cups of water
- 2 tbsp vinegar rice
- 1 tsp of salt
- 2 seaweed sheets nori
- ¼ peeled & sliced lengthwise cucumber
- 2 pieces of crab legs imitation
- ½ package of sliced cream cheese
- 1 tsp fresh minced ginger root

INSTRUCTIONS

1. Over high heat, bring water & rice to a boil in a pot with a lid. Stir often until the rice is cooked & your liquid has absorbed about 20-25 mins. Reduce heat & cover. Salt & rice vinegar should be added at this point. Allow it to cool before removing it from the heat source.

2. Put down a sheet of seaweed. Spread your rice evenly over each sheet, allowing a half-inch space down one side, lengthwise, using your hands. Straighten up the gap by lining up slices of imitation crab meat, cucumber, & cream cheese inside the straight line. Roll your sushi from the uncovered end of your seaweed sheet to the topped end.

3. Slice every roll into 5 or 6 pieces with a wet knife. Minced ginger may be used as a garnish.

NUTRITION

Calories 444 Kcal
Carbs 80 g | Fat 8 g
Protein 10 g

CUCUMBER SUSHI PARCELS WITH SMOKED SALMON

- Prep Time — **60 MIN**
- Cooking Time — **45 MIN**
- Servings — **6**

INGREDIENTS

- 1 standard quantity Sushi Rice
- 6 to 8 sprigs of fresh dill
- 2 Japanese cucumbers
- Salt
- 4 slices of smoked salmon (about 3 oz/80 g total), cut into bite-size pieces
- 18 small capers for garnish

NUTRITION

Calories 291 Kcal
Carbs 51 g | Fat 5 g
Protein 10 g

INSTRUCTIONS

1. Prepare the Sushi Rice. Finely chop the dill and mix it gently into the rice.

2. Rinse the cucumbers, rub them generously with salt and roll them back and forth under your hand on a cutting board so that the salt penetrates them, which helps to heighten their green color. Rinse them again, and then slice them lengthwise into ribbons with a vegetable peeler and set them aside. Each cucumber should make about a dozen ribbons for a total of 24.

3. Lay 2 slices of cucumber closely side by side, with another 2 slices perpendicular to them. The 4 slices should overlap in a woven pattern. For best results, work on the plates on which you plan to serve the sushi.

4. Divide the rice into 6 equal portions. Fill a Japanese teacup or similar rounded container that is about 3 inches (7.5 cm) wide with half of one portion of the Sushi Rice. Press the rice lightly into place and lay a few pieces of salmon on it before covering it with the other half of the rice portion. (To keep rice from sticking, rinse the cup first or line it with plastic wrap.)

5. Turn the rice and salmon cake out onto the center of the woven cucumber. Fold the ends of the cucumber ribbons over the top of the rice to cover it completely.

6. Repeat the process for each of the remaining portions of rice, and garnish with capers.

FISH

CURRY SALMON SUSHI STACKS

Prep Time — **15 MIN**
Cooking Time — **40 MIN**
Servings — **2**

INGREDIENTS

- 1 cup Rice Short Grain
- 2 tbsp vinegar rice wine
- ¼ tsp of each granulated sugar & salt
- 2 cups shredded cooked salmon
- 1/3 cup curry sauce Madras
- 1 avocado ripe, peeled & sliced, halved, pitted
- ½ cup mango diced
- ½ cup cucumber diced
- ¼ cup red onion diced
- ¼ cup divided lime juice
- 1 tbsp fresh ginger minced
- ½ tsp salt
- ½ cup of mayonnaise
- 1 tsp powder curry
- 2 tbsp sesame seeds toasted

INSTRUCTIONS

1. Follow package instructions for cooking the rice. Make a paste using vinegar, salt, & sugar. Let it cool down to room temperature before moving on.

2. Stir the curry sauce into the salmon in a mixing bowl. To taste, salt and pepper are all you need to add to an avocado, mango, and cucumber salad. Set aside a bowl & whisk mayonnaise, the rest of the lime juice, & the curry powder.

3. Divide the salmon mixture, avocado salad, & rice into six individual servings. Salmon mix, avocado salad & rice are layered into a 125 g dry measure; compress the items gently before inverting them onto a serving platter.

4. Keep on until you've used up all of the ingredients. Add a dash of curry mayo & sesame seeds to finish.

NUTRITION

Calories 341 Kcal
Carbs 16 g | Fat 24 g
Protein 28 g

GRILLED EEL SUSHI

- Prep Time — **60 MIN**
- Cooking Time — **40 MIN**
- Servings — **4**

INGREDIENTS

- 1/2 standard quantity Basic Sushi Rice
- 1 grilled eel (unagi kabayaki) with sauce
- 1 oz (30 g) green beans, cooked and cut into 2-in (5-cm)-long strips for garnish
- 4 fresh sansho leaves (or other tiny leafed herbs) for garnish

River Ribbon Garnish (Optional)

- 1 fresh spring roll wrapper (about 8 in/20 cm square)
- Oil for deep-frying

Homemade Kabayaki Sauce

- 2 tablespoons sake
- 3 tablespoons mirin
- 1 1/2 tablespoons sugar
- 3 tablespoons soy sauce

NUTRITION

Calories 444 Kcal
Carbs 80 g | Fat 8 g
Protein 10 g

INSTRUCTIONS

1. Cook the Sushi Rice as per instructions.

2. Divide the rice into 4 portions, & shape each portion into a disk-like platform using a moistened 10-cm open-ended circular kitchen mold.

3. To make the optional River Ribbon Garnish, cut the spring roll wrapper into four long strips. Fold each strip in half along its longer axis & fold it in half again the same way for a long, narrow shape. With scissors or a knife, make a series of cuts at about 1.25-cm intervals along one side of each strip. Repeat the process on the other side of each strip so the cuts on either side alternate. Heat oil to 175°C. Unfold each strip and briefly deep-fry until lightly browned, using chopsticks to gently stretch them out into a lattice shape as they cook. Drain them on a paper towel.

4. Bottled Kabayaki Sauce is available, to make your own, simply combine the sake, mirin, sugar & soy sauce in a pan & simmer over low heat for 5 minutes or until slightly thickened.

5. If the eel is not precooked, brush it lightly with Kabayaki Sauce and grill it over an open flame for a minute or two on each side. Cut the eel into four long strips, and cut these into 2.5-cm squares. Place on a plate and microwave for one or two minutes until they are warm. Arrange the warm eel pieces on top of the rice.

6. Decorate with the green beans, the Kabayaki Sauce, the River Ribbon Garnish, if using, and the sansho leaves or other fresh herbs.

FISH

INSIDE-OUT SPICY TUNA & AVO SUSHI

- Prep Time — **30 MIN**
- Cooking Time — **26 MIN**
- Servings — **2**

INGREDIENTS

Sushi Rice

- 66g sushi-style rice
- 78 ml of water
- 2 & ¼ tsp vinegar rice
- 2 & ¼ tsp sugar white
- 15 g of salt

Sushi Rolls

- 4 oz yellowfin tuna sashimi-grade
- 1/3 cup of mayonnaise
- 35 ml chili oil
- 15 ml oil sesame
- 15 ml sauce sriracha
- 1 diced green onion
- 3 cut into half sheet's nori
- ½ small thinly sliced ripe avocado
- ¼ cut in matchsticks English cucumber

INSTRUCTIONS

1. Make sure the rice is well-cleaned. You can use a sieve, for best result.

2. Bring the rice and water to a boil in a saucepan. About 20 minutes later, turn the heat down to low, cover the pot, and let the rice simmer for another 10 minutes.

3. Put a small saucepan on low heat; whisk sugar & salt to dissolve; 1-2 mins. Combine sugar mixture & rice vinegar. Rice should seem dry after it has cooled and been stirred well.

4. Combine mayonnaise, sriracha sauce, sesame oil, & green onion using a fork in a bowl, mashing to split up the pieces of tuna. Allow a few bits to remain for visual appeal.

5. Using plastic wrap, protect a rolling bamboo mat. Lay a single nori sheet on the mat, with the glossy side down, and press it firmly into place. Cover the nori with a coating of rice. Spread the rice with avocado slices on top of it. It's time to flip your nori sheet. Lay down about 3/4 of the nori sheet with tuna mixture, followed by cucumber matchsticks.

6. Sushi is rolled up using a rolling mat, and the ends are tucked up using plastic wrap. Put sushi roll upon platter after removing plastic wrap. To make more sushi, repeat the process with the rest of the ingredients.

NUTRITION

Calories 749 Kcal
Carbs 38.6 g | Fat 59.4 g
Protein 7.2 g

JAPANESE OMELET SUSHI

Prep Time — **60 MIN**

Cooking Time — **30 MIN**

Servings — **12**

INGREDIENTS

- 3 eggs
- 1 tablespoon mirin
- 15 -30 g of sugar, to taste
- Pinch of Salt
- 15 ml vegetable oil
- 12 nigiri rice balls
- Twelve (1 by 15-cm) nori strips
- Soy sauce for dipping

INSTRUCTIONS

1. Beat the eggs. Add the mirin, sugar and salt and mix well.

2. Heat a rectangular Japanese omelet pan until hot. Add a little of the oil and carefully wipe away the excess with a paper towel, leaving the pan barely slick. Add 1 / 5 of the egg mixture, spreading it evenly over the bottom of the pan. When it is almost set, use a spatula to bunch up the egg at the end of the pan.

3. Push the cooked egg back to the far side of the pan, oil the pan again and add another 1 / 5 of the egg mixture, spread evenly over the visible portion of the bottom of the pan. When the egg has been set, roll the previously cooked portion of the egg across it toward your side as if rolling it up on a carpet. Oil the pan and repeat the same process until all of the egg mixtures are used up.

4. Place the cooked omelet on a bamboo mat and roll it up to form an oval shape. When cooled, cut into slices between about 1 / 4 and 1 / 2 inch (8 mm) thick.

5. Prepare the nigiri rice balls.

6. Top each rice ball with one slice of omelet. Use the nori strips as "belts" to hold the sushi together.

NUTRITION

Calories 218 Kcal
Carbs 30 g | Fat 6 g
Protein 9 g

FISH

CAULIFLOWER TUNA SUSHI ROLLS

- Prep Time — **45 MIN**
- Cooking Time — **15 MIN**
- Servings — **3**

INGREDIENTS

- 1 lb cut in florets cauliflower
- 5 oz softened cream cheese
- 1 tbsp vinegar rice
- 3 tsp sugar substitute monk fruit
- 6 oz cubed ahi tuna sushi-grade
- 1 hot sauce dash Sriracha
- 3 dry seaweed sheets nori
- 1 peeled, pitted, & sliced medium avocado
- 2 tbsp seeds sesame

INSTRUCTIONS

1. Food processors are great for chopping up cauliflower florets and making them into rice.

2. Put the steamer insert into the saucepan, fill it with water until it reaches just below its rim, and remove it from the heat. Bring the water to a rolling boil in a large pot. About 10 mins after putting in the cauliflower, cover the pot and let it steam, stirring regularly.

3. Add the rice vinegar, cream cheese, & sweetener to the cauliflower rice inside a bowl. Refrigerate for an hr or until completely cool.

4. Combine the diced tuna plus Sriracha to your preferred spice level in a separate dish.

5. It would help if you had a square about the size of a nori sheet after spreading 1/3 of your cauliflower mix on a wooden rolling mat wrapped in plastic wrap.

6. Place a single nori sheet over the top of the cauliflower rice square. Layout one-third of avocado slices and one-third of your tuna mix on the nori. Begin by putting the fillings on the outside of the dough and then rolling it up. Cut the roll into six pieces and top with the remaining third of the sesame seeds. Repeat this process with the leftover cauliflower rice, tuna mixture, avocado slices, nori, & sesame seeds.

NUTRITION

Calories 407 Kcal
Carbs 20 g | Fat 30 g
Protein 22 g

MAKI SUSHI WITH BAKED FISH

Prep Time — **40 MIN**
Cooking Time — **15 MIN**
Servings — **2**

INGREDIENTS

- 2 oz salmon sushi-grade
- 1 avocado
- 1 seaweed nori
- 6 oz sushi rice cooked
- 1 tsp of wasabi
- soy sauce
- rice flour
- 6 ozs skinless mackerel
- 2 lettuces
- salt
- sesame oil
- chili sauce
- sesame seeds black & white

INSTRUCTIONS

1. Remove the pit by slicing the avocado in half. A spoon works well for scooping meat from the skin. Slice into quarter-inch wide strips. Slice the salmon into equal-sized pieces.

2. The nori should be placed in the work area. Spread your sushi rice onto the nori sheet using moistened hands. Spread a thin strip of wasabi over the middle of the rice using your finger. Place the avocado slices on top of the Wasabi, then the salmon. The nori should be sprayed with some water to keep it from drying out. Using the lower side of the nori, roll it around the filling. Apply a small amount of pressure to the moistened edge to seal it. 12 equal-sized pieces of salmon roll

3. Pat the mackerel dry and then cut it into 12 pieces that are roughly equal in size. Dredge throughout rice flour and season with a little salt. Fry for a few seconds until golden brown in hot sesame oil. Place a sliver of lettuce on the salmon roll before adding the mackerel. Sesame seeds & chili or soy sauce are excellent dipping accompaniments.

NUTRITION

Calories 321 Kcal
Carbs 16 g | Fat 26 g
Protein 28 g

MANGO & CURRY SALMON STACKS WITH SUSHI RICE

Prep Time — **25 MIN**
Cooking Time — **20 MIN**
Servings — **2**

INGREDIENTS

- 1 cup Grain Rice Short
- 2 tbsp vinegar rice wine
- ¼ tsp each granulated sugar & salt
- 2 cups shredded cooked salmon
- 1/3 cup curry sauce Madras
- 1 ripe halved, pitted avocado, peeled & sliced
- ½ cup mango diced
- ½ cup cucumber diced
- ¼ cup red onion diced
- ¼ cup divided lime juice
- 1 tbsp fresh ginger minced
- ½ tsp salt
- ½ cup of mayonnaise
- 1 tsp powder curry
- 2 tbsp sesame seeds toasted

INSTRUCTIONS

1. Follow the package instructions for cooking the rice. Let it cool down to room temperature before moving on. Add salt & sugar to the vinegar and mix.

2. Toss the salmon with the curry sauce in a small bowl. Toss avocado, red onion, mango, cucumber, ginger, lime juice, & salt in a large bowl. Set aside the mayonnaise mixture and the leftover lime juice & curry powder in another bowl.

3. Make six servings of each: salmon combination, avocado salad, and rice. Layer salmon mix, avocado salad, & rice in a 1-cup dry measure, squeezing contents gently to compress them, then invert upon a serving platter.

4. Keep on until you've used up all of the ingredients. Add a dash of curry mayo & sesame seeds to finish.

NUTRITION

Calories 264 Kcal
Carbs 6 g | Fat 14 g
Protein 15 g

MARINATED FISH SUSHI

- Prep Time — **60 MIN**
- Cooking Time — **80 MIN**
- Servings — **4**

INGREDIENTS

- 1/2 standard quantity Basic Sushi Rice
- 2 horse mackerel, sea bream or red snapper fillets, deboned
- 20 g of salt
- 1 cup (120 g) fresh or frozen soy beans pods or 1/2 cup (85 g) shelled soy beans
- 1/2 cup (125 ml) vinegar
- 2 shiso leaves sliced into threads for garnish

Horse Mackerel Marinade

- 2 tablespoon rice vinegar
- 1 tablespoon sugar
- 6 ozs skinless mackerel
- 2 lettuces
- salt
- sesame oil
- chili sauce
- sesame seeds black & white

NUTRITION

Calories 197 Kcal
Carbs 35 g | Fat 4 g
Protein 5 g

INSTRUCTIONS

1. Prepare Basic Sushi Rice. Sprinkle the fish fillets with salt on both sides, using about 15 g total. Leave them in a flat container for 30 minutes. (If the air in your kitchen is above 20°C, leave the salted fish in the refrigerator.

2. If using fresh soybeans, remove the pods from any branches, wash them off and put them in a pan. Sprinkle the pods with 1 teaspoon of salt and let them stand for a few minutes. Pour hot water over them and boil them on the stove until the beans are tender about 5 minutes. In the case of frozen beans or peas, simply thaw them out and remove the pods. Mix the beans into the rice.

3. Put half a cup of vinegar into a bowl and use it to wash the salt off of the fillets. Do not discard the vinegar.

4. Prepare the Horse Mackerel Marinade by mixing the vinegar and sugar in a flat-bottomed container. Marinate the fish fillets for at least 30 minutes (or as long as a day in the refrigerator). When you are ready to make the sushi, peel the skin off the fillets, starting from the head end. Cut the fish diagonally into slices.

5. Wet a round, open-ended kitchen mold about 4 inches (10 cm) in diameter and place it in the center of a serving plate. Fill it with 1/4 of the rice and bean mixture and press lightly to create a flat surface. Remove the mold and arrange one-quarter of the sliced fish on top of the rice. Decorate with a quarter of the thinly sliced shiso threads, and repeat the process with the remaining ingredients on three more plates.

FULL SEA SUSHI

- Prep Time — **60 MIN**
- Cooking Time — **30 MIN**
- Servings — **2-3**

INGREDIENTS

- 1 standard quantity Basic Sushi Rice
- 4 oz (100 g) fresh tuna, cut into sashimi slices
- 1/2 tablespoon soy sauce
- 6 to 8 fresh whole ama-Ebi shrimp or 3 medium-size shrimp
- 3 fresh scallops
- 1 oz (30 g) tobiko (flying fish roe) or salmon roe
- A few kaiware daikon sprouts or broccoli sprouts, cut into small pieces

Wasabi Dressing Sauce

- 3 tablespoons rice vinegar
- 1/2 teaspoon sugar
- 1 1/2 tablespoons soy sauce
- 1 tablespoon vegetable oil
- 1 teaspoon freshly grated wasabi or wasabi paste

NUTRITION

Calories 444 Kcal
Carbs 80 g | Fat 8 g
Protein 10 g

INSTRUCTIONS

1. Prepare the Basic Sushi Rice.
2. Slice the tuna, preferably sashimi-style & dip one side of each slice in the soy sauce in a small bowl or saucer to give the fish the lightest possible coat of the sauce.
3. Carefully wash, shell & drain the ama-Ebi sweet shrimp. Using medium-size shrimp, shell & devein them and then boil them until just done. Then cut each medium-size shrimp in half lengthwise. Cut each scallop in half—into two discs of even thickness, not two semicircles.
4. Place the Basic Sushi Rice on a serving platter. Arrange the seafood and tobiko attractively on top of it and sprinkle it with the sprouts.
5. Prepare the Wasabi Dressing Sauce by mixing the rice vinegar, sugar, soy sauce, vegetable oil and wasabi. Serve the sushi with the sauce on the side.

PAELLA SUSHI

- Prep Time — **30 MIN**
- Cooking Time — **30 MIN**
- Servings — **4-6**

- 1 tablespoon olive oil
- 2 tablespoons finely minced onion
- 3 oz (80 g) coarsely chopped tomatoes

INGREDIENTS

- 2 cups (400 g) of uncooked rice
- 8 mussels
- 5 medium shrimp
- 1 medium squid, body about 8-in (20-cm) long, head and legs removed
- 2 cups (500 ml) chicken stock
- 1 teaspoon saffron Heaping
- 1/2 teaspoon salt
- 1/2 red bell pepper
- 1/2 green bell pepper
- 1 medium onion, diced
- 1 lemon, cut into wedges
- 2 tablespoons fresh chopped parsley
- Tomato Dressing
- 2 tablespoon white wine vinegar
- 1 tablespoon lemon juice
- 1 1/2 teaspoons sugar
- 1/2 teaspoon salt
- 2 tablespoons water

NUTRITION

Calories 341 Kcal
Carbs 16 g | Fat 24 g | Protein 28 g

INSTRUCTIONS

1. Rinse the rice until the water runs clear, and then soak it for at least 30 minutes. Place the live mussels in a pot or bowl of fresh water for at least 20 minutes. During this time, they should naturally expel any sand or dirt inside. After removing them from the water, cut or pull off their stringy beards and scrub away any other external dirt.

2. Devein the shrimp. Clean the squid, pulling out the stiff, translucent cuttlebone and thoroughly rinsing the interior. Then peel off the membranous skin. (Start by making a knife incision where the fins or "wings" meet the body.) Cut the squid's tubular body into rings about 1/4 -inches (6 mm) thick.

3. Bring the stock to a boil in a paella pan or a skillet, and add the saffron and salt. Add the drained rice, stir, and arrange the mussels, shrimp, squid rings and vegetables on the surface of the rice.

4. Cover the pot and cook for 10 minutes over low heat. Remove the pot from the heat and let it stand, covered for 5 minutes. Sprinkle with the chopped parsley.

5. Mix all the ingredients for the Tomato Dressing, being sure to add them in exactly the order they are listed. Serve the paella with the sauce on the side.

RICE & QUINOA PRAWN SUSHI BOWL

- Prep Time — **10 MIN**
- Cooking Time — **20 MIN**
- Servings — **2**

INGREDIENTS

- 100 g sushi rice brown or white
- 20 g mixed quinoa colored
- 1 & ½ tbsp vinegar rice wine
- ½ tbsp caster sugar golden

For the toppings

- 1 tsp oil
- ½ thinly sliced sweet potato
- 8 large, cooked, peeled prawns
- ¼ finely sliced cucumber
- ½ thinly sliced avocado
- Goma Wakame
- sriracha mayonnaise & sesame seeds

INSTRUCTIONS

1. Cook the rice & quinoa in a large pot medium heat. At boiling point, cover the pot and lower the heat down to the lowest setting possible. For the water to be absorbed, cook for 12-15 minutes or as instructed by the package.

2. Meanwhile, combine vinegar, sugar, & salt in a saucepan & bring to a boil. Gently swirl the rice around to release steam after stirring in the vinegar mixture. When the rice has cooled, it should be tacky rather than wet.

3. Add oil to a non-stick pan & heat it. Sweet potatoes may be fried for 2-3 minutes on each side until they're just done, then cooled and seasoned. The rice may be divided into two small dishes and leveled after cooling.

4. Arrange the other ingredients over the prawns after halving them lengthwise. If desired, serve with a zigzag drizzle of spicy mayo & sesame seeds.

NUTRITION

Calories 439 Kcal
Carbs 61 g | Fat 10 g
Protein 22 g

RESTAURANT-STYLE RAW FISH SUSHI

- Prep Time — **15 MIN**
- Cooking Time — **15 MIN**
- Servings — **6**

INGREDIENTS

For cooking sushi rice

- 1.5 cups sushi rice white
- 2 cups of Water
- ¼ cup Vinegar Rice

For making sushi

- 6 sheets of seaweed sushi
- 250 g salmon raw
- 120 g sliced Cream Cheese
- 1 large sliced avocado

INSTRUCTIONS

1. Add water & white rice sushi to a rice cooker and bring it to a boil. The cooking time should be about 15 minutes. Add the rice vinegar to a cooker after the rice has done cooking and it has cooled down a little. A ladle or big spoon may be used to agitate the mixture well.

2. Lay the seaweed out on a bamboo mat. Then, spread the sushi rice on top of it. Spread the rice out equally. Then, top the rice with salmon, cream cheese, and avocado slices.

3. The bamboo mat and its contents should be rolled up. Make sure the mat is securely rolled. Cut your sushi rolls with a sharp knife now. Add soy sauce on a platter and serve immediately.

NUTRITION

Calories 245 Kcal
Carbs 13 g | Fat 19 g
Protein 23 g

FISH

SALMON SUSHI SALAD

- Prep Time — **15 MIN**
- Cooking Time — **10 MIN**
- Servings — **1**

INGREDIENTS

- 100 g rice sushi
- 50 g edamame beans frozen
- 1 tbsp oil sesame
- 1 torn sheet nori
- pomegranate seeds handful
- 50 g salmon smoked
- 1 small peeled & sliced avocado, stoned
- 1 tsp sesame seeds black
- sushi ginger

For the dressing

- 1 tsp oil vegetable
- 2 tsp molasses pomegranate
- 1 tsp sauce soy

INSTRUCTIONS

1. Rinse the sushi rice thoroughly and place it in a small pot topped with 200 ml of cold water. Simmer for 10 minutes with the cover on after bringing it to a boil. For 15 minutes after removing from the heat, maintain the cover on the pot.

2. While the rice is cooking, place the edamame in a bowl and cover it with hot water to thaw. Combine all dressing ingredients, then store them in an airtight container.

3. Using a nonstick skillet, heat sesame oil and add some nori. Cook for 1-2 minutes over a moderate flame until crispy.

4. Drizzle pomegranate seeds & salmon on top of the edamame and rice before serving. Sprinkle the sesame seeds over the avocado slices and arrange them in a decorative pattern on top. If desired, the dressing may be drizzled over and garnished with sushi ginger slices.

NUTRITION

Calories 862 Kcal
Carbs 87 g | Fat 43 g
Protein 27 g

SHRIMP AND SALMON SUSHI ROLLS

Prep Time — **30 MIN**
Cooking Time — **30 MIN**
Servings — **8**

INGREDIENTS

For sushi rice:

- 2 cups sushi rice short grain
- 2.5 cups of water
- ¼ cup vinegar rice
- 2 tablespoons of sugar
- 1 teaspoon salt

For sushi rolls:

- 1 cucumber medium
- 1 avocado
- 4 jumbo shrimp cooked
- 4 oz cold salmon smoked
- 5 full nori sheets (seaweed)
- sesame seeds Black & white
- Wasabi & soy sauce

NUTRITION

Calories 197 Kcal
Carbs 35 g | Fat 4 g
Protein 5 g

INSTRUCTIONS

MAKE SUSHI RICE:

1. Under cold running water, rinse the rice until the water is clear.

2. To remove the extra water, just drain and shake. To get the appropriate texture, the rice-to-water ratio is critical.

3. Then, bring water to your boil in a saucepan & add the washed rice. Make sure the rice is evenly distributed beneath the water. Set the temperature to medium-high and secure the lid. Bring to a rolling boil.

4. Once the water has come to a boil, turn the heat down to low and cover the pot for 10 minutes. After then, turn off the heat and leave it for the next 10 minutes. Make sure the lid isn't always open.

5. Cooking time will depend on how long it takes for the seasoning to dissolve into the sugar in the rice vinegar thoroughly, so start by preparing the rice seasoning first.

6. Set away for later. Take a big bowl and pour the rice into it after it's done cooking.

7. Sprinkle the rice with the spice mixture. Use a cutting & folding motion with a wooden spatula to carefully combine the ingredients. The idea here is to equally distribute the spice all through the rice & to chill the rice rapidly.

8. While the rice is cooking, it will get more sticky. In this case, you don't want to end up with mashed rice. Don't be too harsh!

FISH

9. Then cover it with a moist kitchen towel while preparing the other ingredients.

PREPARE NORI SHEETS & FILLINGS:

10. If desired, the nori sheets may be crisped up in a pan over the open flame; this step is not required.

11. Cut nori sheets in half to make two rectangular sheets if using whole ones.

12. Cut and slice the fillings into thin strips before using.

MAKE THE ROLLS:

13. Prepare the bowl filled with cold water to keep your hands from drying out as you work with the rice. The rice will not stick to your hands as a result of this.

14. Use a big Ziplock bag to keep the rice off the sushi mat. Arrange everything in and around the work area.

15. Rough side up, place the seaweed sheet on the sushi mat that has been prepared.

16. Wet your hands and distribute the sushi rice evenly over the nori sheet, leaving approximately 1/2 inch from the top. Don't crush the rice this time around. The goal is to keep the rice fluffy and airy.

17. Fillings may be arranged in any way you wish.

18. Roll up the mat and place the thumbs underneath the fillings. Continue rolling until you reach the end of the nori, keeping the fillings in place with the other fingers. The seam should be on the bottom. Don't press too hard when gently squeezing the roll from the bottom up. Squeeze it gently yet firmly to get the desired form.

19. Using a seaweed sheet, lay out the rice evenly, add some sesame seeds & turn the whole thing over. The next step is to lay out the contents on your nori sheet. And much like the prior roll, as well. To form the roll, carefully slide your fingertips over the bottom & the top without pressing too firmly.

20. Using a sharp knife, moisten the blade with water and cut the rolls cleanly. Run the knife through the rolls in a sawing motion without smashing them. Before and after each cut, use a clean moist cloth to clean the knife.

21. Cut sushi rolls and arrange them on a serving tray. For dipping, combine soy sauce & wasabi in a small bowl.

SPICY TUNA SESAME ROLL

Prep Time — **60 MIN**
Cooking Time — **20 MIN**
Servings — **8**

INGREDIENTS

- 1 / 2 standard quantity Basic Sushi Rice
- 3 tablespoons white sesame seeds, roasted
- 3 1 / 2 oz (85 g) fresh tuna, chopped
- 1 teaspoon chili paste
- Dash of soy sauce, or to taste
- Chervil or parsley for garnish

INSTRUCTIONS

1. Prepare the Basic Sushi Rice.

2. Cover a bamboo mat with plastic wrap. Shape the Basic Sushi Rice into an 8-inch (20-cm)-long bar in the center of the mat. Roll the mat up and tighten it to make the bar's thickness even.

3. Sprinkle the sesame seeds on a plate, and roll the bar of rice back and forth over the seeds until it is well coated. Cut the bar into 8 pieces and lay them on their sides on a serving plate.

4. Put the tuna, chili paste and soy sauce in a food processor and process until smooth. Top each sesame-coated portion of rice with a dollop of the spicy tuna paste. Garnish with chervil or parsley.

NUTRITION

Calories 218 Kcal
Carbs 30 g | Fat 6 g
Protein 9 g

SHRIMP RICE PILAF SUSHI

- Prep Time — **30 MIN**
- Cooking Time — **30 MIN**
- Servings — **2**

INGREDIENTS

- 2 cups (400 g) of uncooked rice
- 12 medium shrimp
- 2 cups (500 ml) of water
- 1 tablespoon curry powder
- 1/2 teaspoon salt
- 1/2 cup (75 g) green peas
- 1 tablespoon lemon juice
- 4 sprigs of fresh coriander (cilantro)

Shrimp Marinade

- 3 tablespoons plain yogurt
- 1 teaspoon curry powder
- 1/2 teaspoon garam masala
- 1 teaspoon salt

Yogurt Sauce

- 1/2 cup (125 g) plain yogurt
- 1 tablespoon of sugar
- 1/2 tablespoon ketchup
- 1/2 teaspoon cumin
- 1/2 teaspoon curry powder
- 1/2 teaspoon salt
- 1 teaspoon sugar (optional)

INSTRUCTIONS

1. Wash the rice, and soak it for at least 30 minutes. Drain.
2. Wash, shell and devein the shrimp.
3. Prepare the Shrimp Marinade by mixing the yogurt, curry powder, garam masala and salt. Marinate the shrimp in this mixture for about 10 minutes.
4. In a pan, combine the water with curry powder and salt. When it comes to a boil, add the rice and peas. Stir, cover the pot, and bring it to a boil again. Remove the shrimp from the marinade and add them to the rice pot. (Do not stir them in—just let them cook on the surface of the rice.) Cover, reduce heat to its lowest setting, and cook for 10 minutes.
5. Prepare the Yogurt Sauce by mixing all of the ingredients in a bowl. Depending on the sourness of the yogurt you are using, you may want to add a little less or a little more sugar.
6. When the rice is done, take out the shrimp and set them aside. Gently mix the lemon juice into the rice. Serve the rice on a plate, with the shrimp arranged on top. Garnish it with the coriander and serve the Yogurt Sauce on the side.

NUTRITION

Calories 481 Kcal
Carbs 105 g | Fat 2 g
Protein 10 g

SHRIMP ROLLS

- Prep Time — **60 MIN**
- Cooking Time — **30 MIN**
- Servings — **2**

INGREDIENTS

- 1 standard quantity Basic Sushi Rice
- 8 to 10 fresh medium-size shrimp, heads removed
- Dash of Salt
- 4 tablespoons sake
- 2 tablespoons wasabi paste (vary to taste)
- Soy sauce for dipping

INSTRUCTIONS

1. Prepare the Basic Sushi Rice.

2. Insert a toothpick lengthwise through each shrimp to prevent it from curling up while cooking. Place the shrimp in a saucepan with the sake and salt. Cover and cook over medium heat for 1 to 2 minutes until done.

3. When the shrimp are cool enough to handle comfortably, remove the toothpicks and shell the shrimp. Make a deep incision along the shrimp's undersides so that you can open them up and flatten them out like a hinge or a book.

4. Cover a bamboo mat with plastic. Put half of the sushi rice on the plastic and shape it into an 8-inch (20-cm)-long bar in the center of the mat. Roll the mat up and tighten it to make the bar's thickness even. Unroll it and set the rice bar on a cutting board.

5. Dab a bit of wasabi along the top of the rice bar. Arrange about half of the flattened shrimp neatly on the rice bar, placing them at a 45-degree angle to the bar. Cover with plastic wrap and a bamboo mat, and use these to shape and slightly flatten the bar. Try not to press straight down on the sushi. Instead, as with the Rainbow Roll, exert pressure along the bottom edges of the mat so that it pulls the shrimp downward onto the rice and gives the top of the roll a smooth surface.

6. Remove mat. Cut into bite-size pieces through plastic wrap. Remove the wrap and serve.

7. Repeat with the remaining rice and shrimp to make a second roll.

NUTRITION

Calories 354 Kcal
Carbs 80 g | Fat 8 g
Protein 10 g

FISH

SHRIMP SUSHI

- Prep Time — **40 MIN**
- Cooking Time — **40 MIN**
- Servings — **5**

INGREDIENTS

- 2 cups of sushi rice
- 3 cups of water
- 50 ml vinegar rice
- 50 g sugar
- 1 tsp salt
- 5 seaweed sheets nori
- 1 cut strips carrot
- 1 cut, in strips cucumber
- 1 boiled pack of frozen peeled shrimp
- soy sauce
- wasabi

INSTRUCTIONS

1. Gently rinse the rice unless the water runs clear.
2. Rice should be soaked for around 30 mins in a medium-sized pot with some water.
3. Using moderate heat and a tight-fitting cover, cook your rice for around 15 mins.
4. Turn the heat down and leave the cover on for the next 15 minutes after simmering for 15 minutes.
5. Place rice on serving plate to cool after this.
6. If part of the rice gets stuck to the pan, normal.
7. To make rice sauce, combine vinegar, sugar, & salt in medium saucepan & cook over low heat, constantly stirring, until the sugar is dissolved.
8. Slowly drizzle sauce into rice, swirling & blending.
9. Prepare kitchen counter & ensure ingredients are on hand. The following included: rice, ice, water, seaweed, carrots, cucumbers, and a mat.
10. Place mat in work area w/ bag over top. Open bag & place Nori sheet on it w/ its rough side up.
11. Wet hands w/ cold water & grab handful of rice to eat w/ hands. Spread it out on Nori sheet, leave a room at end for fingers to work with. Few prawns, few carrots, few cucumbers, 4-5 x sheet.
12. Press firmly on mat as you roll up like dough log.
13. Suggested number of equal slices is 8.
14. After each cut, wipe the blade off with a paper towel. It's best served chilled and garnished with a little Japanese sauce.

NUTRITION

Calories 190 Kcal
Carbs 92 g | Fat 5 g
Protein 13 g

SMOKED MACKEREL MAKI ROLLS

Prep Time — **20 MIN**
Cooking Time — **25 MIN**
Servings — **4**

INGREDIENTS

- 150 g rice sushi
- 2 tsp wine vinegar rice
- 4 sheets nori
- 1 deseeded red chili
- ½ peeled carrot
- ¼ cucumber
- 100 g skin removed smoked mackerel
- for dipping soy sauce

INSTRUCTIONS

1. Using your hands, mash the rice inside a small dish of cold water to remove any starch. Drain and rinse until the water is clear, then repeat.

2. Place the rice in a pot with a tight-fitting cover and bring it to a boil over medium-high heat. Ten minutes of simmering in 2.5 cm of water with the cover on are all that is needed. Remove the pot from the heat and cover with a lid for the next 15 minutes. Pour the vinegar into the mixture, then allow it to cool fully.

3. Lay down a sushi mat and fill a small basin with ice water. Over the sushi mat, lay a nori sheet shiny side down. Leave a 1 cm margin just at the top when spreading out a 1/4 of the grains just on the nori.

4. At the bottom of the rice, arrange a fourth of the carrots and chilies. Along the center of the plate, arrange a 1/4 of cucumber and mackerel.

5. For sealing the roll, apply a little amount of water to the top of the roll. Use your sushi mat for rolling up one maki after folding the bottom side of the seaweed over 1st layer of filling. Four rolls may be made by repeating this process twice. Cut every roll into 8 equal halves using a sharp knife. Serve with a side of soy sauce.

NUTRITION

Calories 218 Kcal
Carbs 30 g | Fat 6 g
Protein 9 g

SMOKED SALMON CANAPÉ

- Prep Time — **15 MIN**
- Cooking Time — **10 MIN**
- Servings — **4**

INGREDIENTS

- 4 strips of smoked salmon
- 4 rice-filled canapé cups
- 4 tiny sprigs of fresh dill
- 1/2 mango, thinly sliced
- 4 small pieces of lemon peel
- 4 rice-filled canapé cups
- 4 sprigs of fresh mint

INSTRUCTIONS

1. Roll up each strip of salmon to form a rose. Place one salmon rose on each canapé and garnish with the dill and lemon peel, mango and mint canapé.

2. Arrange the mango slices on the four rice-filled cups and garnish with fresh mint.

NUTRITION

Calories 238 Kcal
Carbs 31 g | Fat 2 g | Protein 12 g

SOFT-SHELL CRAB SUSHI ROLL

- Prep Time — **20 MIN**
- Cooking Time — **20 MIN**
- Servings — **6**

INGREDIENTS

- 1 cup sushi rice cold cooked
- 1 dry seaweed sheet nori
- 1 tbsp of masago
- ½ soft-shell crab deep-fried
- 3 sliced bell pepper red
- 2 leaf lettuce leaves
- ½ tbsp okonomiyaki sauce
- ½ thinly sliced avocado

INSTRUCTIONS

1. Spread half of the nori sheet with rice. Sprinkle the rice with masago. Place the nori on a sushi mat and wrap it up.

2. Onomiyaki sauce is a must, as well as crab and bell pepper. Make a sushi roll by sprinkling nori on top of the other ingredients. Place avocado slices over top of your sushi roll, now cover using plastic wrap & press on again by rolling within the sushi mat. Peel back the wrap by slicing the roll into six equal pieces. Drizzle extra okonomiyaki sauce over the sushi.

NUTRITION

Calories 106 Kcal
Carbs 13 g | Fat 4 g | Protein 3 g

SMOKED SALMON SUSHI ROLL

- Prep Time — **4 H 30 MIN**
- Cooking Time — **30 MIN**
- Servings — **6**

INGREDIENTS

- 2 cups sushi rice Japanese
- 6 tbsp wine vinegar rice
- 6 dry seaweed sheets nori
- 1 peeled, pitted & sliced avocado
- 1 peeled & sliced cucumber
- 8 oz salmon smoked
- 2 tbsp paste wasabi

INSTRUCTIONS

1. Soak the rice for four hr. Drain the rice and add water to a rice cooker. Adding vinegar will need that the rice is dry.

2. Add 6 tbsp of rice vinegar to the heated rice when it's finished cooking. To cool down the rice, spread it out on a platter until fully dry.

3. Press a small coating of chilled rice onto one seaweed sheet on a bamboo mat. Leave at least a half-inch of the seaweed's top and bottom edges exposed. It will make it simpler to seal afterward. Sprinkle some wasabi on top of the rice before serving. The rice should be garnished with cucumbers, avocados, and smoked salmon. Keep them about an inch away from the seaweed's bottom border.

4. The seaweed's top edge should be dampened. Using a bamboo mat, roll the dough firmly from the edge. Serve the roll by slicing it into 8 evenly sized pieces. Repeat this process for the rest of the rolls.

NUTRITION

Calories 291 Kcal
Carbs 45 g | Fat 6 g
Protein 11 g

SPICY CRAB ROLL

- Prep Time — **15 MIN**
- Cooking Time — **45 MIN**
- Servings — **24 PIECES**

INGREDIENTS

For Sushi Rice

- 1 cup short-grain sushi rice
- 1 cup of water
- 1 & ½ tbsp vinegar sushi

Spicy Mayo

- 3 tsp of mayonnaise
- 1 & ½ tsp sauce sriracha

For the Spicy Kani Roll

- 4 oz crab meat Kani
- 2 seaweed sheets nori
- 2 tbsp seeds sesame

INSTRUCTIONS

MAKE SUSHI RICE

1. Put the rice within the rice cooker once it has been rinsed. After that, add water & cook.

2. Once the food has cooled, put it in a big bowl. Mix with sushi vinegar while it's still heated (or the mix of sugar, rice vinegar, and salt).

MAKE YOUR SPICY SRIRACHA MAYO

3. Mix Sriracha sauce & mayonnaise in a transparent dish. If you want it hotter, taste it and add extra Sriracha.

MAKE YOUR SPICY CRAB SALAD

4. Use two forks or hands to shred your crab imitation. Mix in the Sriracha mayo well.

MAKE YOUR SPICY CRAB ROLL

5. With a pair of kitchen scissors, split each nori sheet lengthwise. Place a nori sheet over your bamboo mat with the glossy side down.

NUTRITION

Calories 39 Kcal
Carbs 7 g | Fat 1 g
Protein 1 g

6. Over the nori, evenly distribute the seasoned sushi rice (approximately 3/4 cup). Gently knead the rice with your fingertips. Over the top of your rice, scatter sesame seeds.

7. Make sure the rice side is facing down when you flip the sheet. Fill half of the nori sheet with spicy Kani crab salad.

8. Lift the edge of the bamboo mat up & over your filling with your thumbs. Press both rice & filling together with the bamboo mat as you roll it away from you. Keep rolling till the ends are concluded.

9. Cut the roll into eight equal halves on a cutting board. Add a little spicier mayo sauce on the top of the roll if you'd like.

TUNA AVOCADO SUSHI RICE SALAD

Prep Time — **60 MIN**

Cooking Time — **30 MIN**

Servings — **2-3**

INGREDIENTS

- 1 standard quantity of Brown Sushi Rice
- 4 oz (100 g) fresh, sashimi-quality tuna
- 1 tablespoon soy sauce
- 1/2 tablespoon sesame oil
- 1/2 avocado, cut into small cubes
- 1 bunch of kaiware daikon or broccoli sprouts

INSTRUCTIONS

1. Prepare the Brown Sushi Rice.
2. Cut the tuna into small, bite-size slices and marinate for at least 10 minutes in the soy sauce and sesame oil.
3. Gently mix the tuna and avocado into the Brown Sushi Rice. Turn it into a plate and sprinkle with sprouts.

NUTRITION

Calories 346 Kcal
Carbs 47 g | Fat 11 g
Protein 13 g

SPICY TUNA SUSHI ROLL

- Prep Time — **85 MIN**
- Cooking Time — **20 MIN**
- Servings — **4**

INGREDIENTS

- 2 cups white rice uncooked glutinous
- 2 & ½ cups of water
- 1 tbsp vinegar rice
- 1 can solid drained white tuna
- 1 tbsp of mayonnaise
- 1 tsp powder chili
- 1 tsp paste wasabi
- 4 dry seaweed sheets nori
- ½ finely diced cucumber
- 1 finely diced carrot
- 1 peeled, pitted & diced avocado

INSTRUCTIONS

1. Over high heat, bring the water, rice, & vinegar to a boil. Stir sometimes unless your rice is cooked and some liquid has been absorbed for about 20-25 minutes. Lower, bring to a simmer & cover. Around 10 mins later, remove the lid and let the extra water drain out of the sponge. Prepare and chill the rice.

2. Make a light sauce by combining the tuna with the mayonnaise, chili powder, & wasabi paste, but do not overdo it.

3. Wrap the bamboo sushi roll mats with plastic before rolling the sushi. Lay a piece of nori on top of the plastic wrap, with the rough side facing up. Cover the nori with a thick, even coating of rice that is firmly patted down with damp fingertips. Diced carrot, cucumber, & avocado should be placed in a line down the bottom of a sheet, & the tuna mix should be spread out beside the veggies.

4. Begin by picking up one of the rolling bamboo sheets and folding it up to enclose the sushi's contents. Then roll it up into a long, thick tube. It is necessary to carefully compress tightly compacted sushi after the roll is wrapped within the mat. Each roll should be cut into six pieces and refrigerated until serving.

NUTRITION

Calories 346 Kcal
Carbs 47 g | Fat 11 g
Protein 13 g

SUSHI CRAB SALAD RECIPE

- Prep Time — **2 MIN**
- Cooking Time — **15 MIN**
- Servings — **2**

INGREDIENTS

- 1 cup rice sushi
- ½ pound crab meat cooked
- 1 cucumber small
- ½ sliced avocado
- 2 roasted seaweed sheets
- 2 chopped scallions
- 1-inch grated ginger
- 1 grated clove garlic
- 1 tablespoon mustard Dijon
- 3 teaspoons sauce soy
- ¼ cup cider vinegar apple
- 1 juiced lemon
- ½ cup olive oil extra virgin

INSTRUCTIONS

1. To prepare sushi rice, follow the directions on the box. In a bowl, add sushi rice and mix well.
2. Add crab, avocado, cucumbers, toasted seaweed, & scallions to the rice. If desired, top with sesame seeds.
3. Make the dressing by combining all the ingredients in a bowl & whisking them together until smooth.
4. Enjoy your rice dish with some dressing on top.

NUTRITION

Calories 289 Kcal
Carbs 23 g | Fat 15 g
Protein 7 g

SUSHI EEL EGGROLLS W/ CREAM CHEESE

Prep Time — 60 MIN
Cooking Time — 40 MIN
Servings — 10

INGREDIENTS

- 1 standard quantity Basic Sushi Rice
- 4 oz (100 g) grilled eel with Kabayaki Sauce
- 2 oz (50 g) cream cheese, cut into 1/4-in (6-mm) dice
- 10 Egg Sheets
- 10 tiny sprigs of sansho leaves for garnish (optional)

INSTRUCTIONS

1. Prepare the Basic Sushi Rice.
2. Japanese eels almost always come precooked. In this case, cut it into small pieces and allow it to marinate in its own sauce.
3. If the eel is not precooked, grill it over an open flame for a few minutes on each side, brushing it lightly with Kabayaki Sauce. When it is done, cut it into small pieces.
4. Mix the eel and the cream cheese with the Basic Sushi Rice. Divide the rice mixture into 10 portions and gently form them into oval-shaped rice balls.
5. Place a rice ball in the middle of an Egg Sheet, flatten it slightly, and wrap it neatly. Repeat with the remaining rice balls and Egg Sheets.
6. Optionally, garnish with tiny sprigs of sansho leaves or other fresh herbs.

NUTRITION

Calories 232 Kcal
Carbs 23 g | Fat 14 g
Protein 3 g

THAI SHRIMP SUSHI PARCELS

- Prep Time — **60 MIN**
- Cooking Time — **20 MIN**
- Servings — **2-3**

INGREDIENTS

- 1 standard quantity Basic Sushi Rice
- 4 to 5 oz (about 125 g) fresh small shrimp, shelled and deveined
- Dash of Salt
- 1 tablespoon sake
- 1/2 teaspoon chili sauce
- 1 teaspoon fish sauce, preferably Thai (nam pla)
- 2/3 cup (60 g) finely diced pineapple (either fresh or canned)
- 2 tablespoons roasted and finely chopped cashew nuts
- 4 or 5 fresh lettuce leaves
- 1 fresh chili pepper, thinly sliced
- 4 or 5 sprigs of fresh coriander (cilantro)

INSTRUCTIONS

1. Prepare the Basic Sushi Rice.
2. In a microwave-safe dish, combine the shrimp, salt and sake. Cover the dish with plastic wrap and microwave it for a few minutes until the shrimp are just done. Drain the shrimp, but reserve 1 tablespoon of the liquid.
3. Add the chili sauce and fish sauce to the liquid from the shrimp. Mix it into the Basic Sushi Rice.
4. Add the pineapples and cashew nuts to the rice and mix gently but thoroughly.
5. Line several small serving bowls or other small containers with the lettuce leaves and turn the rice out into them.
6. Top each of the rice "parcels" with the cooked shrimp and garnish them with sliced chili pepper and fresh coriander.

NUTRITION

Calories 289 Kcal
Carbs 23 g | Fat 15 g
Protein 7 g

TOKYO-STYLE SUSHI RICE SALAD

Prep Time — 60 MIN

Cooking Time — 45 MIN

Servings — 4-6

INGREDIENTS

- 2 standard quantities of Basic Sushi Rice
- 4 1/2 oz (125 g) fresh tuna, cut into 1/2-in (1.25-cm) cubes
- 1 1/2 teaspoons soy sauce
- 1 tablespoon sake
- 2 pinches of Salt
- 5 oz (150 g) fresh or frozen shrimp, shelled and rinsed
- 3 eggs
- 1 tablespoon mirin
- 1 1/2 to 2 tablespoons sugar, or to taste
- 4 or 5 sprigs of mitsuba, cut into 1-in (2.5-cm) lengths

INSTRUCTIONS

1. Prepare the Basic Sushi Rice.
2. Marinate the tuna in the soy sauce for 5 minutes.
3. Prepare the shrimp by cooking them sakamushi style—that is, steamed in sake. Pour just enough sake to cover the bottom of a pan—about a tablespoon—plus a little water and a pinch of salt.
4. Add the shrimp and bring the pot to a boil. Reduce the heat to its lowest setting and cook, covered, for a few minutes until the shrimp have a nice pink color.
5. You may also microwave the shrimp for 2 minutes with 1 tablespoon of sake in a dish covered with plastic wrap. After the shrimp are cooked, cut them into 1/2-inch (1 cm) pieces.
6. Use the eggs, mirin, sugar and 1 pinch of salt to prepare a Japanese omelet.
7. When finished, cut the omelet into 1/2-inch (1-cm) cubes.
8. Mix the tuna, shrimp and omelet cubes into the Basic Sushi Rice. Turn into a serving dish and sprinkle with the mitsuba stems.

NUTRITION

Calories 232 Kcal
Carbs 23 g | Fat 14 g
Protein 3 g

TRADITIONAL NORI TUNA ROLLS

Prep Time — **60 MIN**
Cooking Time — **10 MIN**
Servings — **4**

INGREDIENTS

- 2 sheets nori
- 1 teaspoon wasabi paste
- 4 oz (100 g) fresh uncooked tuna, cut into 7-in (18-cm)-long and 1/2-in (1.25-cm)-thick bars

INSTRUCTIONS

1. Prepare the Basic Sushi Rice and divide it into four equal portions.

2. Cut each nori sheet in half across its longer length. This should give you four pieces of approximately 4 by 7 inches (10 by 18 cm) each.

3. Place one piece of nori with its shiny side down on a rolling bamboo mat, with one of the nori's longer sides lined up with the near edge of the mat. Spread one portion of Basic Sushi Rice gently and evenly across the nori, leaving about 1 inch (2.5 cm) of nori exposed at the far edge.

4. Spread 1/4 of the wasabi sparingly across the center of the rice. Place a single long bar of tuna across the rice on top of the wasabi. (If no one piece of tuna is long enough, you may place shorter pieces end to end.)

5. Use the mat to roll up the nori with the rice and tuna inside. Once the sushi is rolled up, firmly grasp the rolled mat and gently tug it on its free end to make sure the roll is tight. Unroll the mat and put the rolled sushi on a cutting board.

6. Slice the roll into pieces 1 to 1 1/2 inches (2.5 to 3.75 cm) thick. Repeat the process with the rest of the nori and Basic Sushi Rice to make four rolls.

NUTRITION

Calories 291 Kcal
Carbs 50 g | Fat 5 g
Protein 10 g

TUNA SALAD ROLLS

- Prep Time — **60 MIN**
- Cooking Time — **10 MIN**
- Servings — **4**

INGREDIENTS

- 1 standard quantity Basic Sushi Rice
- 2 sheets nori
- 1 small can of tuna in oil, about 3 oz (80 g)
- 2 tablespoons minced onion
- 2 tablespoons mayonnaise
- Dash of freshly ground black pepper

INSTRUCTIONS

1. Prepare the Basic Sushi Rice.
2. Cut each nori sheet in half across its longer length. This should give you four pieces of approximately 4 by 7 inches (10 by 18 cm) each.
3. Drain excess oil from the tuna. To prepare the tuna salad, mix the tuna with the minced onion, mayonnaise and pepper.
4. Divide the Basic Sushi Rice into 4 equal portions. Place one piece of nori with its shiny side down on a rolling bamboo mat, with one of the nori's longer sides lined up with the near edge of the mat. Spread one portion of Basic Sushi Rice gently and evenly across the nori, leaving about 1 inch (2.5 cm) of nori exposed at the far edge.
5. Use the mat to roll up the nori with the rice and tuna salad inside. Once the sushi is rolled up, firmly grasp the rolled mat and gently tug it on its free end to make sure the roll is tight. Unroll the mat and put the rolled sushi on a cutting board.
6. Slice the roll into pieces between 1 to 1 1/2 -inches (2.5 to 4 cm) thick. Repeat the process with the rest of the nori and Basic Sushi Rice to make a total of four rolls.

NUTRITION

Calories 346 Kcal
Carbs 47 g | Fat 11 g
Protein 13 g

TUNA FILLET RICE SALAD

- Prep Time — **60 MIN**
- Cooking Time — **30 MIN**
- Servings — **4-6**

INGREDIENTS

- 2 standard quantities of Basic Sushi Rice
- 2 oz (50 g) drained Pickled Ginger
- 1 bonito tuna fillet or other tuna fillets (about 8 to 10 oz/300 g)
- 2 tablespoons soy sauce
- 2 tablespoons mirin
- 2 tablespoons gold or white sesame seeds, roasted
- 8 spring onions or thin green onions (scallions), finely chopped

INSTRUCTIONS

1. Prepare the Basic Sushi Rice.
2. Cut the ginger pickles into thin matchsticks. Add them to the rice and mix gently.
3. Cut the bonito fillets into small bite-size pieces, about 1/4-inches (6 mm) thick. Marinate the fish in the soy sauce and mirin for about 10 minutes.
4. Add the bonito and its marinade to the rice. Sprinkle it with the sesame seeds and most of the spring onions and mix thoroughly but gently.
5. Serve the mixed sushi in bowls, sprinkling on the remaining chopped onion as garnish.

NUTRITION

Calories 346 Kcal
Carbs 47 g | Fat 11 g
Protein 13 g

TUNA TARTARE GUNKAN SUSHI

- Prep Time — **60 MIN**
- Cooking Time — **20 MIN**
- Servings — **8**

INGREDIENTS

- 4 1/2 oz (125 g) fresh tuna
- 2 teaspoons soy sauce
- 2 tablespoons roasted and finely chopped walnuts
- 2 spring onions, chopped
- 8 nigiri rice balls
- 8 strips of nori, cut to about 1 1/4 by 6 in (3 by 15 cm)
- Soy sauce for dipping

INSTRUCTIONS

1. Chop or mince the tuna and mix in the soy sauce. Add the walnuts and onions. 2 Make the nigiri rice balls.

2. Wrap one strip of nori around each rice ball to form a small cup, with the nori on the sides of the cup and the rice on its floor. To keep the ends of the nori strips from flapping loose, you may secure them with a dab of "glue" made by crushing grain or two of Basic Sushi Rice between your fingers.

3. Use a spoon to fill each cup with the tuna, onion and walnut mixture.

NUTRITION

Calories 346 Kcal
Carbs 47 g | Fat 11 g
Protein 13 g

TWO-CHEESE TUNA SALAD ROLLS

- Prep Time — **60 MIN**
- Cooking Time — **30 MIN**
- Servings — **2**

INGREDIENTS

- 1 standard quantity of Simple White Rice
- 1 tablespoon lemon juice
- 1 small can of flake tuna in oil (about 3 oz/80 g)
- 2 tablespoons finely minced onion
- 2 tablespoons mayonnaise
- Dash of black pepper
- 5 or 6 sprigs of fresh parsley
- 4 sandwich slices of American cheese
- 4 sandwich slices of cheddar-style cheese

INSTRUCTIONS

1. Prepare the Simple White Rice.
2. Add lemon juice to the cooked rice. Mix gently but thoroughly.
3. Prepare the tuna salad by draining the excess oil from the canned tuna. Mix the tuna with onion, mayonnaise and pepper.
4. Place a sheet of plastic wrap on a bamboo mat on a board. Divide the rice into two portions and spread one of them evenly on the plastic wrap, forming a rectangle of about 5 1 / 2 by 8 inches (14 by 20 cm).
5. Arrange half of the tuna salad across the center of the rice. Place half the parsley on top of the salad. Roll the sushi and tighten it with a mat.
6. Take the rollout of the mat and place it on a cutting board. Cut each of the cheese slices in half for a total of 16 pieces. Arrange 8 of the pieces on top of the rolled rice, positioning them at a slight angle to the roll. The pieces should slightly overlap, with colors alternating.
7. Cover the sushi with plastic wrap and a mat. Gently press to form the rounded shape of the roll. Remove the mat and cut the roll into slices through the plastic wrap. Remove the wrap before serving. Repeat with the remaining ingredients to make a second roll.

NUTRITION

Calories 218 Kcal
Carbs 30 g | Fat 6 g
Protein 9 g

BARBECUED PORK INSIDE-OUT ROLLS

- Prep Time — **60 MIN**
- Cooking Time — **30 MIN**
- Servings — **2**

INGREDIENTS

- 1 standard quantity Basic Sushi Rice
- 1 1/2 teaspoons vegetable oil plus more for boiling the peppers
- 1/2 yellow bell pepper, cut into strips
- 1/2 green bell pepper, cut into strips Salt and pepper
- 6 oz (180 g) pork loin, thinly sliced
- 1 tablespoon sake
- 1 tablespoon sugar
- 1 tablespoon vinegar
- 1 tablespoon soy sauce
- 2 tablespoons tomato ketchup
- 1 tablespoon black sesame seeds, roasted
- 3 or 4 frilly lettuce leaves or other salad greens, torn into very small pieces

INSTRUCTIONS

1. Prepare the Basic Sushi Rice.
2. Boil a pan of water with a few drops of vegetable oil added. Add the yellow and green peppers and boil for 15 seconds until barely tender. (In this way, the vegetable is cooked to a glossy finish with fewer calories than if it had been sautéed.) Drain.
3. Warm a skillet and add 1 1/2 teaspoons of oil. Lightly sprinkle salt and pepper over the pork and stir-fry it until the color of the pork changes. Add the sake, sugar, vinegar, soy sauce and ketchup and cook for 1 minute, stirring constantly. The sauce should thicken slightly.
4. Mix the sesame seeds into the Sushi Rice. Divide the rice into two portions.
5. On a board lay a sheet of plastic wrap over a bamboo mat. Spread one portion of sushi rice on the plastic to form a 6 by 8 inch (14 by 20 cm) rectangle.
6. Arrange half of the lettuce across the center of the rice. Top with half of the cooked pork and pepper mixture. Roll the mat tightly to make a roll.
7. Repeat with the remaining ingredients to make another roll. Cut the two rolls into slices to serve.

NUTRITION

Calories 444 Kcal
Carbs 80 g | Fat 8 g
Protein 10 g

BARBECUE HOT DOG SUSHI ROLL

Prep Time — **45 MIN**
Cooking Time — **30 MIN**
Servings — **2**

INGREDIENTS

- 1 cup of water
- 1 cup sushi rice short grain
- 1 tbsp vinegar rice
- 1 hot dog all-beef
- 1 dry seaweed sheet nori
- 1 tbsp red onion diced
- ¼ cup divided barbecue sauce
- ¼ cup divided Cheddar cheese shredded
- 2 tbsp onions French-fried

NUTRITION

Calories 629 Kcal
Carbs 98 g | Fat 19 g
Protein 12 g

INSTRUCTIONS

1. In a big saucepan, bring 1 cup of water & rice to a boil. Simmer the rice for 15 mins with the heat down to low and the lid on. Remove from the heat and rest for approximately 10 mins until the water has been absorbed. Rice should be seasoned with vinegar. Using a 1/3 cup of measure, put the sushi rice in the refrigerator for approximately 30 mins to chill down.

2. Boil some water in a medium saucepan. Add a hot dog and lessen the heat. Simmer for around 5 mins until the food is heated completely.

3. The plastic wrap should be placed on a level surface. Set up a nearby cup of hot water. Place your nori 2 inches away from its edge, nearest your body, facing inward. Spread your rice evenly over nori with damp fingertips. A single inch separates the bottom of the rice & nori from the hot dog. Next to the hot dog, arrange the onions in a row. Top each hot dog with 2 tsp of barbecue sauce. Top with 2 Tbsp of Cheddar cheese.

4. Gently peel the nori from the plastic wrap by grabbing the edge closest to you. Pulling just on plastic wrap, firmly roll your sushi into a thick cylinder, enclosing the contents with a fold-over. Take off the plastic wrap. Moisten your fingertips with warm water and gently pat its edge close with your fingers to seal the nori.

5. Using a sharp knife, slice the sushi roll into six equal pieces. Serve the slices straight off the cutting board on a plate. The remaining 2 tsp of barbecue sauce & 2 tbsp of Cheddar cheese should be included. French-fried onions may be added as a garnish.

BEEF CELERY SUSHI RICE SALAD

- Prep Time — **60 MIN**
- Cooking Time — **30 MIN**
- Servings — **2-3**

INGREDIENTS

- 1 standard quantity of Brown Sushi Rice
- 4 1/2 oz (125 g) beef loin, thinly sliced
- 1 stalk celery (or ½ burdock root)
- 1 tablespoon peeled and minced fresh ginger
- 2 tablespoons mirin
- 2 tablespoons soy sauce
- 1 1/2 tablespoons sugar
- 2 spring onions or thin green onions (scallions), chopped

INSTRUCTIONS

1. Prepare the Brown Sushi Rice.
2. Cut the beef slices into small pieces. Cut the celery into thin slices. In a pan, combine the ginger, mirin, soy sauce and sugar.
3. Add the celery and cook for 1 minute. Add the beef and cook until all the liquid is absorbed.
4. Mix the beef and vegetables into the rice. Turn it into a serving dish and sprinkle it with the chopped spring onions.

NUTRITION

Calories 862 Kcal
Carbs 87 g | Fat 43 g
Protein 27 g

BUFFALO CHICKEN SUSHI

- Prep Time — **25 MIN**
- Cooking Time — **25 MIN**
- Servings — **4**

INGREDIENTS

- ½ lb breaded tenderloins chicken breast fully cooked
- ¼ cup pepper sauce hot
- 4 dry seaweed sheets nori
- 4 cups sushi rice cooked
- 1 peeled & cut into 4" matchsticks carrot
- 1 cut into 4" matchsticks celery stalk
- ¼ cup mayonnaise spicy
- ¼ cup onions French-fried

INSTRUCTIONS

1. Cook the chicken in a large bowl with the spicy sauce, turning it to coat it well.

2. Sushi mats made of bamboo work well for nori sheets. Leave a ½-inch strip of nori along one side for spreading 1 cup of rice. The chicken, carrots, and celery should be arranged along the rice's edge.

3. Roll all ingredients firmly around the mat, using the edge closest to the filling as a guide. Apply a little amount of water to the edge of your nori & press for sealing; repeat the rest of the ingredients.

4. Sharp, moist knife: Slice every roll into 8 pieces. Top every piece using a little quantity of French-fried onion & dollop of mayonnaise.

NUTRITION

Calories 522 Kcal
Carbs 54 g | Fat 26 g
Protein 14 g

CHICKEN RICE SUSHI

- Prep Time — **40 MIN**
- Cooking Time — **30 MIN**
- Servings — **4-5**

INGREDIENTS

- 2 cups (400 g) of uncooked rice
- 2 boneless chicken thighs, about 1 to 1 1/2 lbs (450 to 700 gr.)
- Salt
- One 4-in (10-cm)-long piece long onion (naganegi), chopped
- 3 thin slices of fresh ginger
- 2 1/2 cups (625 ml) water
- 2 tablespoons lemon juice
- 1/2 cucumber, finely diced
- 4 sprigs of fresh coriander (cilantro)
- 4 lemon wedges

Chili Sauce

- 7 oz (200 g) stewed tomatoes
- 4 tablespoons vinegar
- 3 tablespoons sugar
- 1/2 to 1 teaspoon dried red pepper flakes
- 1 teaspoon soy sauce

NUTRITION

Calories 473 Kcal
Carbs 76 g | Fat 48 g
Protein 8 g

INSTRUCTIONS

1. Thoroughly wash the rice, rinsing it until the water runs clear, and then soak it in water for at least 30 minutes. Drain.
2. Trim excess fat from the chicken. Cut the meat to a uniform thickness for even cooking. Sprinkle the chicken with salt.
3. Place the chicken, chopped onion, ginger and water in a pot and bring to a boil. Cover the pot, lower the heat and let it simmer for 15 minutes until done. Set the chicken aside to cool and strain the broth.
4. In a pan, bring 2 cups (500 ml) of the broth and 1/2 teaspoon of salt to a boil. Add the drained rice. Stir, cover and bring to a boil once again.
5. Lower the heat and cook for 10 more minutes. Remove from the heat, mix in the lemon juice and the cucumber, and let it stand for 5 minutes.
6. To prepare the Chili Sauce, combine the tomatoes, vinegar, sugar, dried red pepper flakes and soy sauce in a blender or food processor.
7. Puree until smooth, and then pour the mixture into a pan and cook until it is slightly thickened.
8. Serve rice with chicken pieces on top and Chili Sauce on the side. Garnish it with coriander and lemon wedges.

CHICKEN SALAD SUSHI

- Prep Time — **15 MIN**
- Cooking Time — **12 MIN**
- Servings — **12**

INGREDIENTS

- 1/2 standard quantity Basic Sushi Rice
- 1 boneless, skinless chicken breast half
- 1 tablespoon sake Dash of Salt
- 1 teaspoon reserved chicken drippings (from the chicken)
- 2 Japanese cucumbers
- Freshly ground black pepper
- 2 tablespoons minced onion
- 2 tablespoons mayonnaise
- 1 teaspoon lemon juice

INSTRUCTIONS

1. Prepare the Sushi Rice.
2. Lightly sprinkle the chicken with the sake and salt. Microwave for a few minutes until done. Reserve 1 teaspoon of the drippings.
3. Thinly slice the cucumbers into broad ribbons with a vegetable peeler and soak them in cold water for a few minutes to make them crisp. Pat them dry with a paper towel.
4. Divide the rice into 12 portions and make sushi balls.
5. Shred the chicken into tiny pieces and mix them with the onion, mayonnaise, lemon juice and reserved chicken drippings.
6. Wrap a cucumber ribbon around each sushi ball to form a cup, with the cucumber forming the cup's sides and the rice filling most of the interior.
7. Gently flatten the rice at the bottom of the cup with your finger to create a little space for the chicken salad. Fill the cup with a spoonful of chicken salad, sprinkle it with freshly ground pepper, and serve immediately.

NUTRITION

Calories 473 Kcal
Carbs 76 g | Fat 8 g
Protein 48 g

CHICKEN SUSHI

- Prep Time — **20 MIN**
- Cooking Time — **20 MIN**
- Servings — **8**

INGREDIENTS

- 1 & ½ cups rice sushi
- ½ tsp of salt
- 3 tbsp vinegar sushi
- 4 sheets nori
- 1 sushi mat bamboo
- shredded Roast chicken
- 1 stoned, peeled & chopped avocado halved
- 1 cut in thin strips small carrot
- to serve soy sauce
- to serve pickled ginger
- to serve wasabi
- Seriously Heinz Style Mayo is Good Japanese

INSTRUCTIONS

1. Rinse the rice well under cold water in a strainer. Add 2 & ½ cups of cold water & ½ tsp salt to a pot and bring to a boil. Bring to a boil. For almost 12 mins, cover & simmer. Let it cool for 10 mins before removing the cover. Pour with sushi vinegar & let cool on a baking sheet.

2. The lines of the nori should go horizontally across the surface of the bamboo sushi mat. Rice should be distributed over the nori with damp fingertips, leaving a 2 cm strip clear of rice over one side of the sheet.

3. Sliced avocado and carrots are arranged on a rice bed mixed with Heinz Japanese Style Mayo.

4. Use a bamboo mat as a guide to roll your sushi outward from you. Refrigerate for around 30 mins after wrapping with cling film. Repeat the procedure with the leftover ingredients.

5. Slicing and serving with wasabi, soy sauce, & pickled ginger.

NUTRITION

Calories 473 Kcal
Carbs 76 g | Fat 48 g
Protein 35 g8

GRILLED BACON SUSHI ROLL

- Prep Time — **20 MIN**
- Cooking Time — **20 MIN**
- Servings — **4**

INGREDIENTS

- 6 thick bacon slices
- ½ lb ground beef lean
- 1 tbsp spice rub barbecue
- 4 thin prosciutto slices
- 2 sliced jalapeno peppers
- 2 Jack cheese sticks, pepper
- 2 tbsp sauce barbecue
- 1 cup onions French-fried

INSTRUCTIONS

1. On a sushi mat, place two slices of bacon lengthwise.

2. In a medium bowl, combine ground beef & the spice rub. You'll need to leave about an inch of bacon exposed on one end of the bacon for this method to work. Cover the meat with prosciutto. The end nearest to you has a jalapeño strip on it. Sliced jalapenos and cheese sticks go well nicely in this dish.

3. Roll up, neatly and carefully, the exposed end of the bacon.

4. The grill should be preheated at 350 degrees Fahrenheit (175 degs C). Cook the bacon roll, seam side down, for approximately 25 mins on indirect heat. The sauce should be brushed over the top.

5. Continue cooking for another 5 mins or until the barbecue sauce has coated. Grill for a further 5 mins with the remaining barbecue sauce on top, then serve.

6. Remove from the grill, sprinkle with fried onions, and then serve immediately. Chopsticks may be used to serve the food.

NUTRITION

Calories 660 Kcal
Carbs 48 g | Fat 29 g
Protein 21 g

KOREAN KIMCHI SUSHI ROLLS

- Prep Time — **60 MIN**
- Cooking Time — **30 MIN**
- Servings — **4-5**

INGREDIENTS

- 1 standard quantity Basic Sushi Rice
- 1 1/2 tablespoons of dark sesame oil
- 2 oz (50 g) pork loin, thinly sliced
- 2 eggs
- 1/2 cucumber, thinly sliced salt and pepper
- 2 sheets nori
- 3 oz (80 g) kimchi, cut into 1-in (2.5-cm) pieces

INSTRUCTIONS

1. Prepare the Basic Sushi Rice.
2. Add 1 tablespoon of sesame oil to the Basic Sushi Rice. Mix gently but thoroughly.
3. Heat the remaining 1/2 tablespoons of sesame oil in a skillet. Sprinkle salt and pepper on the pork slices, and stir-fry them until the pork turns white.
4. Slightly beat the eggs and add them to the skillet, along with the cucumber. Season the mixture to taste with a little salt.
5. When the egg is nearly done, remove the pan from the heat.
6. Place a sheet of nori on a bamboo mat on a board. Spread 1/2 of the rice evenly on the nori, leaving a 1-inch (2.5-cm) strip of uncovered nori on the side farthest from you.
7. Lightly squeeze or press the kimchi to remove excess water. Arrange 1/2 of the kimchi across the center of the rice.
8. Arrange half of the pork and egg mixture on the kimchi. Roll it up tightly on the mat. Remove the roll from the mat and cut it into slices. Repeat with the remaining ingredients to make another roll.

NUTRITION

Calories 476 Kcal
Carbs 92 g | Fat 5 g
Protein 13 g

ONIGIRAZU

- Prep Time — **30 MIN**
- Cooking Time — **30 MIN**
- Servings — **4**

INGREDIENTS

Onigirazu

- 4 sheets nori
- 4 cups of sushi rice cooked
- 1 sliced avocado
- 25 g spinach, baby
- red cabbage, pickled & shredded
- vegan mayo or Sriracha

Katsu

- 2 pressed chicken thighs
- soy sauce or tamari
- 1 cup of aquafaba
- 1 to 2 cups breadcrumbs panko
- all-purpose cornflour or flour
- 2 cups oil frying

Sweet Potato

- 1 sweet potato large
- 1 tbsp soy sauce or tamari
- 1 tbsp syrup maple
- 2 tsp oil neutral
- 1 tsp sesame oil toasted
- 2 tsp vinegar rice

Quick Pickled Red Cabbage (Optional)

- a wedge sliced thinly red cabbage
- ½ cup vinegar rice
- 2 tbsp maple syrup or sugar
- 1 tsp sea salt fine
- 1 crushed clove of garlic

NUTRITION

Calories 570 Kcal
Carbs 85 g | Fat 16 g
Protein 22 g

INSTRUCTIONS

1. Set your oven to 200 degrees Celsius (390 degrees Fahrenheit) and prepare a baking sheet with parchment paper.

2. Toast your panko breadcrumbs in a pan until they're golden brown and crispy. Using a pair of scissors, slice every chicken thigh in half. Chicken may be seasoned with soy sauce or salt, depending on your preference.

3. Chicken should be dragged into flour to ensure that it is completely covered. To finish, coat the chicken with toasted breadcrumbs & then dip it in the gelatinous aquafaba.

4. Bake the chicken for approximately 30 minutes, rotate the pieces halfway through and brush the baking paper with a touch of oil.

SWEET POTATO VERSION

5. Set your oven temperature to 220°C & line the baking sheet with baking paper. Bake for about

30 mins. In a small bowl, combine the rest of the ingredients. Peel & cut the sweet potato into 12 cm / 0.2" slices from the widest part of the potato.

6. Make sure each slice is coated in the marinade before placing it on the baking sheet. About halfway through the cooking time, rotate the pieces to the other side and continue baking for an additional five mins.

ASSEMBLY

7. Cut a piece of cling film the same size as your nori sheet and place it on top of it. Place your nori sheet over the top of the cling film, glossy side down, then rotate it 45 degrees.

8. Your hands should be wet, so grasp a few grains of rice. Form a tight square with your hands in the center of the sheet after placing it there. Try to level and condense the top layer. Salt your food to taste.

9. On top of it, add the other ingredients. To make the tofu onigirazu, layer spinach, Sriracha, avocado slices, & chicken katsu on top of it. Use a layer of Sriracha, avocado slices, pickled cabbage, & sweet potato disc for sweet potato onigirazu.

10. At this stage, add another layer of crushed rice to cover everything. Getting the rice firmly packed without squashing the things below proved challenging.

11. On a sheet of Al foil that had been gently greased, make a rice layer on top of the stack & then peel the foil off when you are done. A specific onigirazu mold is available to make this process simpler.

12. Seal all 4 corners of the nori sheet over the top of the filling after completing your stack. When you get the right corner folded over the stack, moisten one wet finger & fold your left corner of the stack, 'gluing' it to the right corner. Repeat with the right corner. Repeat the process with the bottom and top corners to make a little package.

13. It's now time to seal up the stack of cling film & tie it all together. Set the onigirazu aside for a few mins to allow the seaweed to soften. Using a sharp knife, halve the piece of fruit.

QUICK PICKLED RED CABBAGE

14. Sterilize a medium-sized jar and add cabbage shreds to it.

15. Add the leftover ingredients to a small pot along with water. Over low heat, bring the mixture to a simmering boil.

16. Pour the hot mixture out over the cabbage & give it a good toss. Check to see that all of the cabbage is covered with pickling juice. Consume after 6-8 hrs in the fridge.

GREEN SUSHI W/ FRESH GOAT CHEESE

- Prep Time — **30 MIN**
- Cooking Time — **25 MIN**
- Servings — **6**

INGREDIENTS

- 1 cucumber
- 1 goat cheese fresh
- 2 tbsp cream sour
- coarse salt or black salt Hawaii
- hazelnut oil
- finely chopped chives

NUTRITION

Calories 372 Kcal
Carbs 61 g | Fat 6 g
Protein 15 g

INSTRUCTIONS

1. Rinse the cucumber. For each side, use a paring knife to make a series of long, thin slices, trying to discard the cucumber's seeds.

2. Mix the goat cheese, chives, and 2 tbsp in a small bowl. Sour cream, salt, and pepper. Stir well.

3. To make this dish, lay 2 cucumber strips into the cross shape on the flared surface and spoon some of your goat cheese mixtures onto one end.

4. Cucumbers should be folded and rolled over to encapsulate the goat cheese.

5. Sprinkle using coarse salt & drizzle with some hazelnut oil. Keeping it in the fridge until you're ready to eat it is recommended.

PEKING DUCK SUSHI

- Prep Time — **60 MIN**
- Cooking Time — **30 MIN**
- Servings — **8**

INGREDIENTS

- 1 standard quantity Basic Sushi Rice
- 1 Japanese cucumber
- 1 1/2 teaspoons vegetable oil
- 1 duck breast or thigh, about 10 oz (300 g)
- 1 tablespoon sake
- 1 tablespoon soy sauce
- 1/2 tablespoon sugar
- 1 tablespoon plus 1 teaspoon mirin
- 1 long onion (naganegi), about 9-in (23-cm) long
- 10 Chinese pancakes or fresh rice paper spring roll wrappers

Sweet Peking Miso Sauce

- 2 tablespoons miso paste or hoisin sauce
- 2 tablespoons water
- 1/2 tablespoon sugar
- 1 teaspoon soy sauce

NUTRITION

Calories 862 Kcal
Carbs 87 g | Fat 43 g
Protein 27 g

INSTRUCTIONS

1. Prepare the Basic Sushi Rice.

2. Using a vegetable peeler, slice several long, flat ribbons from the cucumber. Continue to slice away ribbons until 2/3 of the cucumber is used up. Soak the ribbons in ice water until crisp. Finely dice the remaining cucumber, and mix the diced portion into the Basic Sushi Rice.

3. Heat the oil in a skillet, and brown the skin side of the duck over medium-high heat. When nicely browned, turn the meat over and lower the heat. Cover and cook until done, for about 5 minutes.

4. Add the sake, soy sauce, sugar and 1 tablespoon of mirin to the skillet. Cook the duck over medium-high heat until all the liquid is absorbed, turning the meat several times while cooking. Add the remaining teaspoon of mirin and cook briskly until the duck takes on a nice glossy look. Remove the duck from the heat and allow it to cool.

5. Prepare thin, crisp onion strips (called shiraganegi, meaning "white hair onion," in Japanese) by cutting the long onion into 3-inch (7-cm) lengths. Make a deep vertical cut in each piece and remove the core in the center. Open the onion and flatten it out on a cutting board. Piling a few onion sheets on top of each other, slice them very finely, following the grain. Soak the resulting strips in ice water for a few minutes until crisp. (Note: If you Follow

PINK SUSHI

- Prep Time — **30 MIN**
- Cooking Time — **15 MIN**
- Servings — **6**

INGREDIENTS

- 6 nori sheets
- 1 cup of sliced and stir fried chicken strips and veggies of your choice
- 1 tbsp sesame seeds black
- For Pink Rice
- 1 cup rice sushi
- 1/4 cup vinegar rice
- 1 tbsp of sweetener
- 1 tsp powder beet
- salt

INSTRUCTIONS

the package directions for preparing rice. Serve at room temperature.

6. Sugar, beet powder, and vinegar need to be mixed in a bowl. Add the mixture to a bowl of rice & well stir. Don't break the rice by scraping the surface with your hands. While sticky, dry rice is ideal.

7. Chicken and veggies should be sliced thinly, and nori should be halved.

8. Lay down a quarter sheet of nori on your sushi mat and begin rolling.

9. Spread a little amount of rice on the nori sheet using wet fingertips. At the top, leave a margin of around 2 centimeters.

10. Rice should be topped with your fillings at the bottom.

11. You may begin by rolling your sushi using your hands. Make sure it's securely fastened by pressing hard on both sides. To prevent the filling from escaping, use your fingertips. Seal the roll by brushing water on the edge with wet fingertips. Keep rolling unless it is completely wrapped up.

12. Repeat this process with the leftover nori, rice, & vegetables.

13. Use a knife to cut the rolls into slices. With pickled ginger, wasabi, & soy sauce on the side, serve sushi. Enjoy!

NUTRITION

Calories 356 Kcal
Carbs 43 g | Fat 15 g
Protein 12 g

PORK CUTLET TONKATSU SUSHI

- Prep Time — **60 MIN**
- Cooking Time — **40 MIN**
- Servings — **8**

INGREDIENTS

- 1 standard quantity Basic Sushi Rice
- 1 tablespoon Dijon mustard with seeds
- Salt and pepper
- 1/2 teaspoon vegetable oil
- 8 to 10 fresh lettuce leaves
- 2 cups (500 ml) vegetable oil for deep-frying
- 7 oz (200 g) pork fillets, cut into 10 small pieces
- 1/2 cup (65 g) all-purpose flour
- 1 egg, lightly beaten
- 1 cup (125 g) breadcrumbs

Tonkatsu Sauce

- 2 tablespoons balsamic vinegar
- 2 tablespoons tomato ketchup

NUTRITION

Calories 862 Kcal
Carbs 87 g | Fat 43 g
Protein 27 g

INSTRUCTIONS

1. Prepare Basic Sushi Rice. Add the mustard to the rice and mix well.

2. Boil water in a pan. Add 1 teaspoon of salt and 1/2 teaspoon of vegetable oil. Blanch the lettuce leaves and then immediately soak them in iced water.

3. Drain the leaves and blot excess water from them with a paper towel or tea towel. This process should result in lettuce leaves that are pliable and shiny.

4. Cover a bamboo mat with a sheet of plastic wrap. Arrange half of the lettuce leaves on the mat, overlapping each other to cover an area about 6 inches (15 cm) square, a little smaller than a standard sheet of nori. (To avoid soggy results, be sure there is no excess water on the lettuce.)

5. Arrange half of the rice like a log across the center of the lettuce. Use the mat to roll up the rice inside the lettuce and tighten it to form a firm roll. (Optionally, you may flatten the sides of the rolled-up mat to give the sushi roll a square-shaped cross-section.)

6. Unroll the mat and remove the plastic wrap. Then, drape the roll with plastic wrap and cut it into 5 slices.

7. Repeat with the remaining rice and lettuce to make a second roll.

8. Arrange the sliced sushi on a platter, with a cut side up. Cover it with a thin, damp cloth to keep it from drying out.

9. Start to warm the 2 cups (500 ml) of oil in a deep pan for deep-frying. Cut the pork fillets into 10 small pieces. Sprinkle them with salt and pepper. Dredge them in the flour, then the beaten egg and then the breadcrumbs. Deep-fry the small cutlets in 350°F (175°C) oil for a few minutes until done. Set the meat on a rack or paper towel to allow excess oil to drain.

10. Prepare the Tonkatsu Sauce by mixing together the balsamic vinegar and tomato ketchup in a small bowl. Top each piece of sliced sushi with a petite pork cutlet. Serve with the Tonkatsu Sauce on the side.

SMOKED DUCK SUSHI WITH ORANGE

Prep Time — **15 MIN**
Cooking Time — **10 MIN**
Servings — **8**

INGREDIENTS

- 8 slices of smoked duck breast (about 5 oz/140 g total)
- 8 nigiri rice balls
- 2 teaspoons mustard
- 2 tablespoons minced candied orange peel
- 2 or 3 chives, cut into thin 1-in (2.5-cm)-long strips
- Soy sauce for dipping

INSTRUCTIONS

1. Combine one slice of duck with one nigiri rice ball, substituting 1/4 teaspoon of mustard for the wasabi. Repeat for the remaining pieces of duck and rice.

2. Garnish with orange peel and chives.

NUTRITION

Calories 291 Kcal
Carbs 51 g | Fat 5 g
Protein 10 g

PROSCIUTTO ROLLS

- Prep Time — **45 MIN**
- Cooking Time — **20 MIN**
- Servings — **16**

INGREDIENTS

- 1/2 standard quantity Simple White Rice
- 1/2 tablespoon lemon juice
- 8 slices of prosciutto ham, approximately 4 by 3 inches (10 by 7 cm)
- 2 oz (50 g) blue cheese, crumbled
- 1/2 apple, cut into sticks
- 4 or 5 lettuce leaves, torn into small pieces, for garnish

Walnut Sauce

- 1 tablespoon white wine vinegar
- 1 teaspoon sugar
- 1/2 teaspoon soy sauce
- 1/2 teaspoon olive oil
- 1 tablespoon roasted and finely chopped walnuts

INSTRUCTIONS

1. Prepare the Simple White Rice. Mix in the lemon juice while the rice is freshly cooked and still warm. Divide the rice into 8 portions.
2. Lay a piece of prosciutto flat on a bamboo mat. If its length and width are noticeably different, place it so that it appears vertical to you.
3. Spread one portion of rice on the ham, leaving about 1 inch (2.5 cm) uncovered on edge farthest from you. Arrange 1/8 of the blue cheese and apple sticks across the center of the rice. Roll the ham and rice up carefully and tighten the roll with the mat.
4. Repeat with the remaining ingredients to make eight rolls. Cut each roll in half and arrange them on a plate with some lettuce as a garnish.
5. Prepare the Walnut Sauce by combining the white wine vinegar, sugar, soy sauce and olive oil. Mix thoroughly, and then add the walnuts. Serve the Walnut Sauce alongside the prosciutto rolls for dipping.

NUTRITION

Calories 299 Kcal
Carbs 36 g | Fat 13 g
Protein 8 g

ROAST BEEF ASPARAGUS ROLLS

- Prep Time — **60 MIN**
- Cooking Time — **30 MIN**
- Servings — **2**

INGREDIENTS

- 1 standard quantity Basic Sushi Rice
- 4 tablespoons finely chopped watercress stems
- 3 stalks of asparagus, boiled in salted water
- 5 oz (150 g) thinly sliced roast beef
- 2 teaspoons horseradish
- 5 or 6 watercress leaves for garnish

Fragrant Citrus Sauce

- 2 tablespoons yuzu juice or lemon juice
- 1/2 teaspoon grated yuzu peel or lemon peel
- 2 teaspoons soy sauce
- 1 teaspoon sugar

NUTRITION

Calories 862 Kcal
Carbs 87 g | Fat 47 g
Protein 23 g

INSTRUCTIONS

1. Prepare the Basic Sushi Rice.
2. Mix finely chopped watercress stems w/ the Basic Sushi Rice. Divide into two portions.
3. Place a sheet of plastic wrap over a bamboo mat. Spread one portion of rice to cover a rectangular area 7 inches (18 cm) square. Place half of the asparagus in the center of the rice and roll up the rice around it. Tighten the mat around the roll by holding the rolled-up mat with one hand and gently pulling at the mat's free end with the other. The resulting roll should look like a solid white cylinder of rice.
4. Remove the plastic wrap from the roll and dab a little horseradish all along the top of the roll. Then, layer half of the roast beef diagonally along the length of the roll. Work your way down the roll, placing each piece at the same 45-degree angle to the roll, allowing the pieces to overlap enough to cover the rice.
5. Drape the roll with the plastic wrap again, followed by the bamboo mat. For this step, don't actually roll it again. Instead, leave it upright (beef on top) and apply gentle pressure to the bamboo mat along the bottom of the roll so that the mat pulls the toppings firmly down onto the rice roll and gives the top of the roll a smooth, uniform surface.
6. Repeat to make a second roll.
7. Mix all ingredients for the Fragrant Citrus Sauce, and serve it alongside the rolls. Garnish the top of the rolls with the watercress leaves.

SEARED TATAKI BEEF SUSHI

Prep Time — 15 MIN
Cooking Time — 20 MIN
Servings — 3

INGREDIENTS

- Salt and pepper
- 3 tablespoons sake
- 1 clove garlic, thinly sliced
- 2 tablespoons prepared horseradish
- 10-oz (300 g) beef rump steak, no more than 3 / 4 -in (2-cm) thick
- Bamboo skewers (pre-soaked in water for 30 minutes) (optional)
- 3 tablespoons soy sauce
- 15 nigiri rice balls

INSTRUCTIONS

1. Lightly sprinkle the beef with the salt and pepper. Thread the meat onto skewers and grill it over an open flame. Because this is a relatively large piece of meat, you will probably need three skewers to hold it.

2. Arrange the skewers in a fan shape and hold them at the point all three of them cross. Cook each side of the beef for about 1 minute or until it is done to your preference. Remove skewers and let the meat rest for 15 minutes.

3. As an alternative to this open-flame method, simply sear the beef on both sides in a very hot skillet. Do this for 30 seconds on each side for rare meat, and longer for medium or well-done.

4. Make a sauce by combining the sake, soy sauce and garlic in a saucepan. Bring it to a boil long enough for the alcohol to evaporate from the sake, and then pour it through a strainer. 3 Slice the beef very thinly.

5. Prepare the nigiri rice balls, using the beef in place of fish and about 1 / 2 teaspoon of horseradish in place of the wasabi.

6. Serve the Seared Tataki Beef Sushi with the sauce on the side for dipping.

NUTRITION

Calories 238 Kcal
Carbs 31 g | Fat 2 g
Protein 12 g

ORIGINAL MUSHROOM AND CHICKEN SUSHI RICE

Prep Time — **60 MIN**
Cooking Time — **30 MIN**
Servings — **2**

INGREDIENTS

- 1 standard quantity Basic Sushi Rice
- 1 boneless, skinless chicken breast half
- 4 medium-size eringi mushrooms (about 5-in/12.5- cm long)
- Dash of Salt
- Dash of pepper
- Drizzle of olive oil
- 3 tablespoons minced fresh watercress leaves (tender part)
- 4 sprigs of watercress to garnish
- Zingy Marinade
- 2 tablespoons white wine vinegar
- 1 teaspoon sugar
- 1/2 teaspoon salt
- 1 teaspoon Dijon mustard with seeds

INSTRUCTIONS

1. Prepare the Basic Sushi Rice.
2. Cut any tendons from the chicken and pound the breast to a uniform thickness so that heat will penetrate them even while they are cooking. Cut the mushrooms to 2-inch (5-cm) lengths and then slice those to about 1/8 -inch (3-mm) thick.
3. Arrange the chicken and mushrooms on a metal baking tray and lightly sprinkle them with salt, pepper and olive oil. Broil for several minutes until the chicken is done (when the juice runs clear).
4. As soon as the chicken is cool enough to comfortably handle, shred the meat into small bits. Tear the mushrooms into narrow strips.
5. Prepare the Zingy Marinade by mixing the white wine vinegar, sugar, salt and mustard. Add the chicken and mushrooms, stir them until they are thoroughly coated, and leave them to marinate for about 5 minutes.
6. Gently mix the minced watercress into the Basic Sushi Rice.
7. Pour the marinated chicken and mushrooms over the rice and mix them in gently.
8. Turn the rice into a serving dish and garnish it with fresh green sprigs of watercress.

NUTRITION

Calories 473 Kcal
Carbs 76 g | Fat 8 g
Protein 48 g

SWEET CHILI CHICKEN SUSHI

- Prep Time — **50 MIN**
- Cooking Time — **20 MIN**
- Servings — **24**

INGREDIENTS

- 1 cup rice sushi
- ¼ cup mirin seasoning Obento
- 4 cuts in strips lengthways chicken tenderloins
- ¼ cup chili sauce sweet
- 2 tsp oil rice bran
- 2 tbsp mayonnaise Kewpie
- 4 sheets nori
- ½ thinly sliced medium avocado
- ½ cut into thin strips Lebanese cucumber
- 5 green oak torn lettuce leaves

INSTRUCTIONS

1. Sushi rice may be made by: Rinse & drain the rice three times or until water is completely clear. Set a strainer over a bowl and strain the rice. Drain for ten mins before using.

2. In a small saucepan, combine rice w/ water & bring it to a simmer. Cover. Bring to a boil. Reduce temperature. Cook for 12 mins or unless the water has been absorbed, then remove from the heat. Removing the food from the heat is necessary. For 10min, keep covered.

3. Rice should be transferred onto ceramic dish. Stir the rice with a spatula to break up any lumps. Lift & flip the rice as you gradually add spice until the rice has cooled.

4. In a dish, combine the chicken & 2 tbsp of sweet chili sauce. To finish, put on your coat.

5. Heat oil on medium in large pan, add onion. Add chicken to the mix. Cook for 5 mins on each side or until well heated. Meanwhile, mix mayonnaise & remaining sweet chili sauce.

6. The glossy side of a nori sheet should be facing down on a sushi mat. Spread a quarter of the rice mixture over the nori, leaving a 2 cm strip at one long end, using wet fingertips. In the center of the rice, spread ¼ of the mayonnaise mixture. Rice should be topped with a quarter of a chicken, avocado, cucumber, and lettuce.

7. Form a roll by rolling tightly on a mat. Make 6 slices out of roll. Repeat process with the leftover sheets, avocado, cucumber, mayonnaise, rice, chicken, & lettuce to produce 24 pieces total. Serve.

NUTRITION

Calories 65 Kcal
Carbs 5 g | Fat 3 g
Protein 3 g

TACO SUSHI

Prep Time — **40 MIN**
Cooking Time — **30 MIN**
Servings — **6-8**

INGREDIENTS

- 1 standard quantity of Simple White Rice
- 2 tablespoons lime juice
- 2 oz (50 g) cheese, cut into 1/4-in (6-mm) dice
- 1 1/2 teaspoons olive oil
- 1 clove of garlic, minced
- 1/2 lb (250 g) minced beef
- 4 tablespoons tomato ketchup
- A few drops of Tabasco or other hot sauce to taste
- Salt and pepper to taste
- 3 leaves crisp iceberg lettuce, finely shredded
- 6 to 10 cherry tomatoes, chopped
- 6 to 8 taco shells

INSTRUCTIONS

1. Prepare the Simple White Rice.
2. Add the lime juice to the rice and mix well. Add the cheese and mix well. Divide the rice into 6 to 8 roughly equal portions, depending on the number of tacos you wish to make.
3. Combine the oil and garlic in a pan, and cook over medium heat until the garlic is lightly browned. Add the ground beef and stir until the meat is cooked.
4. Add the ketchup and Tabasco sauce and season with salt and pepper.
5. Spoon one portion of rice into each taco shell, along with some shredded lettuce and cooked beef. Sprinkle the chopped tomatoes on top and serve immediately. Alternatively, arrange the rice, vegetables and meat on a platter and allow your guests to build their own tacos at the table. This will help keep the taco shells crisp until they are ready to be eaten.

NUTRITION

Calories 218 Kcal
Carbs 30 g | Fat 6 g
Protein 9 g

TERIYAKI CHICKEN POUCHES SUSHI

Prep Time — 60 MIN
Cooking Time — 30 MIN
Servings — 10

INGREDIENTS

- 1 standard quantity Basic Sushi Rice
- 10 Inari Tofu Pouches
- 2 tablespoons white sesame seeds
- 2 boneless chicken thighs, about
- 3 / 4 lb (350 g) total
- 1 tablespoon vegetable oil
- 1 tablespoon sake
- 1 tablespoon mirin
- 1 / 2 tablespoon sugar
- 1 1 / 2 tablespoons soy sauce
- 3 spring onions or thin green onions (scallions), cut into 2-in (5-cm) pieces

INSTRUCTIONS

1. Prepare Basic Sushi Rice.
2. Prepare the Inari Tofu Pouches.
3. Sprinkle the white sesame seeds over the Basic Sushi Rice and mix them in. Divide the rice into 10 equal portions. Mold each portion into a ball and put one in each pouch.
4. Fold the edges of the pouch halfway down the inside to make a basket-like rim. The rice inside should fill only about half of the pouch, leaving room for the chicken.
5. To give the chicken skin an attractive brown color, preheat a skillet until it is very hot. Add the oil and put the chicken on the skin side down.
6. Cook over high heat until the skin is nicely browned. Then, turn the chicken over and pour the sake over it. Cover and cook over low heat for about 5 minutes. When the chicken is almost done, add the mirin, sugar, soy sauce and the white parts of the onions.
7. Continue cooking over medium heat, occasionally turning, until the chicken looks nice and shiny.
8. Cut each thigh into small pieces. Place the pieces into the basket formed by the top of each tofu pouch. Decorate with the cooked white parts of the onion, and add a little of the green part as well as a further garnish.

NUTRITION

Calories 473 Kcal
Carbs 76 g | Fat 8 g
Protein 48 g

TERIYAKI CHICKEN SUSHI ROLL

- Prep Time — **45 MIN**
- Cooking Time — **25 MIN**
- Servings — **4**

INGREDIENTS

For rice

- 2 cups rice sushi
- 4 cups of water
- vinegar Rice

For teriyaki chicken

- 1 chicken breast boneless, skinless
- teriyaki sauce Bottled
- oil Sesame
- sugar Brown

For sushi rolls

- 5 seaweed sheets
- 1 diced avocado
- Chicken
- 5 asparagus spears fresh

As a side:

- ginger Pickled
- Sriracha mayonnaise
- Wasabi

NUTRITION

Calories 521 Kcal
Carbs 43 g | Fat 8 g
Protein 34 g

- mayonnaise Sriracha
- onions Fried

INSTRUCTIONS

1. Prepare sushi rice. Use cold water to rinse the rice. Heavy-duty saucepan with water is required. In a medium saucepan, bring water to a boil over medium heat. Cover & bring to simmer.

2. Cook the rice for 15-20 mins or until it is tender but still firm to the bite. Serve after cooling down. Once the rice has cooled, drizzle it with 1-2 tsp of rice vinegar. Assemble the rolls as soon as possible.

3. Make a teriyaki chicken dish. Chicken breasts may be diced into thin slices. In a plastic bag, combine chicken, sesame oil, & a touch of brown sugar with some drops of your teriyaki sauce.

4. Place all ingredients in a zip-top bag and refrigerate for 1 hr to marinate. In a little olive oil, sauté the chicken for 3-4 mins, unless it is cooked through & slightly crispy on the exterior. Take out of the pan and place on a cooling rack.

5. Sushi mats, shiny side down, are spread down the seaweed for sushi rolls. A layer of sushi rice, add a few more ingredients on top (avocado slices, chicken, & asparagus). You don't want the sushi to break apart after you slice it, so begin rolling your sushi from top to bottom; care to maintain the roll tight. Repeat process with all rolls.

6. Cut the rolls once wrapped in plastic wrap and kept in the refrigerator. Slice every roll into eight slices using a sharp knife. On the side, serve ginger & wasabi.

CHICKEN SUSHI DELICACY

🐟 Prep Time — **30 MIN**
🍚 Cooking Time — **50 MIN**
🍴 Servings — **6**

INGREDIENTS

- 1 cup sushi rice short grain
- 2 cups of water
- 1 salt pinch
- 1 & ½ tsp oil vegetable
- ¼ cup vinegar rice
- 2 tbsp sugar white
- 1/8 tsp of salt
- 500g of chicken cut into strips
- 1 tbsp oil olive
- ¼ minced small onion
- 1 tsp minced garlic
- ¼ cup mayonnaise vegan
- 2 tbsp sauce sriracha
- 2 nori sheets
- ½ peeled, pitted, & sliced avocado
- ½ cup Savoy cabbage matchstick-sliced
- ¼ cup carrots matchstick-cut
- ¼ cup seeded cucumber matchstick-cut

INSTRUCTIONS

1. Cook rice with water and salt in a pot until it reaches a rolling boil. A wooden rice spatula or a tiny wooden spoon may be used to stir once. Cover & lower the temperature. In approximately 20 mins, the water will be absorbed, and the rice will be done. Let it cool down.

2. Sugar, Rice vinegar, & 1/8 tsp salt go into a small pot with heated vegetable oil. Heat until sugar dissolves, then remove from heat. When the sugar has melted and the liquid has reached a simmer, remove the pan from the heat.

3. Remove from the heat and let it cool for almost 10 mins before handling. Stir in a tiny amount of a cooled liquid at a time until the rice is moist but not mushy; you might not need the whole amount of liquid.

4. In a small pan, heat the olive oil on medium heat. Cook & stir the chicken until it's golden brown, approximately 4 mins on each side.

5. Prepare a small bowl of mayonnaise & sriracha mixed.

6. Set a sushi mat on a nori sheet with the rough side up. Prepared rice is patted onto the nori with moist fingertips to form a thick and uniform coating that thoroughly covers it. Line the base of your sheet with chicken strips, cabbage, carrots, avocado, and cucumber.

NUTRITION

Calories 299 Kcal
Carbs 36 g | Fat 13 g
Protein 8 g

7. Roll sushi mats and nori sheets over the filling and seal the edges. Using plastic wrap, firmly twist the ends of the roll to compress it. Refrigerate for 5-10 mins to set. Replace nori and fill as necessary.

8. Take off the sushi roll from plastic wrap, cut this into pieces, & then drizzle the sriracha mayonnaise over top them.

CHILI RICE BOWL WITH BEEF & EGG

Prep Time — **15 MIN**
Cooking Time — **20 MIN**
Servings — **2**

INGREDIENTS

- 140 g rice sushi
- 250 g thinly sliced rump steak
- 1 chopped garlic clove
- 1 tbsp sauce soy
- 2 tbsp oil sesame
- sugar
- 2 eggs
- 1 carrot large
- 1 courgette large
- 2 tbsp chili sauce sweet & spicy

NUTRITION

Calories 621 Kcal
Carbs 63 g | Fat 23 g
Protein 41 g

INSTRUCTIONS

1. It should take around eight to ten minutes to cook your sushi rice inside a big pan with lots of water. Cover with lid and store in the refrigerator.

2. Mix your steak with garlic, sugar, soy sauce, and a pinch of black pepper in a medium-sized saucepan. Use two frying pans or a frying pan & a wok to heat the oil to a barely smoking temperature.

3. Set the eggs aside to cool off. Remove the steak from the other pan and keep it heated. Stir-fry the veggies for a minute, then move them to one side of the pan, add the rice, and cook for another minute to heat through.

4. Serve the steak, rice, and vegetables in separate dishes. Dip the eggs in the chili sauce and place them on top. The heated rice & sauce may be tossed together by everyone, ensuring that the egg yolk is evenly distributed.

YAKITORI SUSHI SKEWERS

Prep Time — 60 MIN
Cooking Time — 30 MIN
Servings — 10

INGREDIENTS

- 1/2 standard quantity Basic Sushi Rice
- 10 wooden skewers, at least 6-in (15-cm) long
- 7 oz (200 g) chicken thigh, cut into at least 10 bite-size pieces
- 1/2 long onion (naganegi), cut into 1 1/2 -in (4-cm) pieces
- Dash of ground red pepper (cayenne) for garnish

Yakitori Sauce

- 6 tablespoons mirin
- 6 tablespoons soy sauce
- 4 tablespoons sugar

INSTRUCTIONS

1. Prepare the Basic Sushi Rice.
2. Soak the wooden skewers in water. (This keeps them from burning on the grill later.)
3. Microwave the chicken pieces for 2 minutes until nearly done.
4. Shape the Basic Sushi Rice into 20 round, slightly flattened balls. (One way to do this is to place a bite-size portion of Basic Sushi Rice in a piece of plastic wrap and twist the wrap tightly around it to make a ball, then press on it with your thumb to flatten it slightly.)
5. Arrange the rice balls, long onion and nearly cooked chicken pieces on the skewers. Continue until all are skewered. (Put the skewers through the flattened sides of the rice balls.)
6. Make the Yakitori Sauce by combining the mirin, soy sauce and sugar in a pan and cooking over medium heat until slightly thickened.
7. Grill the yakitori on a barbecue or other hot grill, occasionally turning until the chicken is fully cooked. Brush the skewered ingredients several times with the Yakitori Sauce while cooking.

NUTRITION

Calories 289 Kcal
Carbs 23 g | Fat 15 g
Protein 7 g

VEGETARIAN

VEGGIE SUSHI

Prep Time — **5 MIN**

Cooking Time — **5 MIN**

Servings — **1**

INGREDIENTS

Sushi Rice

- 1 cup white rice medium grain
- 1 cup water
- 2 tbsp rice vinegar seasoned
- 1 tsp of salt

Vegetable Sushi Roll

- 1 nori sheet
- ½-1 tsp seeds sesame
- ¼ cup vegetables
- pickled ginger
- wasabi

NUTRITION

Calories 354 Kcal
Carbs 11 g | Fat 21 g
Protein 35 g

INSTRUCTIONS

WHITE SUSHI RICE

1. Before cooking, a metal mesh strainer may remove any extra starch from the rice. Shake off any extra moisture.

2. To prepare the quick pot: Rinse rice and add salt to it. Add a little bit of water. Add one tsp of salt. Cook for 6 mins on high pressure in an instant pot.

3. Toss rice into a serving dish, and coat it with rice vinegar. Don't smush the rice but fold it gently, and don't overdo it.

VEGETABLE SUSHI ROLL

4. A wooden sushi rolling board should be covered with plastic wrap. Lay down a nori sheet on the mat. To eliminate surplus moisture, wet hands and clap. Keep a bowl full of water & a towel nearby to assist you in cleaning up after a spill.

5. Cover nori with a layer of rice. Approximately one cup of cooked rice per nori sheet is required. Leave a 1-inch margin on the top edge of the nori. Dip your hands into the water when they become a little sticky. Add sesame seeds and thin sliced vegetables.

6. Lift the filling's borders using a bamboo mat. Tuck the roll in with your fingers. Pull back & tighten the mat once it has been rolled up so that only the nori & no rice are visible. Squeeze & shape the mat as you move it around.

7. Cut into thirds, then into thirds again. Keep the knife clean by wiping it down with a moist cloth after every slice.

CUCUMBER SUSHI ROLLS

Prep Time — 15 MIN
Cooking Time — 0 MIN
Servings — 2

INGREDIENTS

Sushi

- 2 diced cucumbers
- 1 cup cooked rice sushi
- ¼ sliced firm avocado
- ¼ red sliced bell pepper
- ¼ orange sliced bell pepper

Spicy Mayo

- 1 tbsp mayonnaise light
- ½ tsp of sriracha

INSTRUCTIONS

1. Allow the rice to cool before stirring it. Everything will stay together better because of the stickier texture.

2. Assemble: Using a tiny knife or spoon, remove your seeds from either side of the cucumber to make a hollow tube.

3. A tiny quantity of rice should be spooned into the tube and then compressed towards one side. When the rice is almost filled, add an avocado slice and several slices of pepper, gently compress & add additional rice to cover the spaces.

4. Slice the cucumber into half-inch-thick slices using a sharp knife. Add extra rice and peppers if the filling comes out of the tortilla during cutting.

5. Spicy mayo or Soy sauce are good options for dipping.

NUTRITION

Calories 207 Kcal
Carbs 37 g | Fat 5 g
Protein 4 g

BUTTERNUT SQUASH ROLLS

- Prep Time — **35 MIN**
- Cooking Time — **70 MIN**
- Servings — **6**

INGREDIENTS

For your Brown Sushi Rice

- 2 & ½ cups of 500 g brown rice long grain
- 4 cups of water 1 liter
- 2/3 cup of 160 ml vinegar rice
- 1/3 cup sorghum or raw honey
- 1 tbsp sugar white
- 2 & ½ tsp sea salt coarse

For your Butternut Squash Roll

- 3 cups Sushi Rice Brown
- 8 oz peeled & deseeded butternut squash
- 2 & ½ cups of vegetable stock with low sodium or Vegetarian Dashi
- 2 cloves garlic
- One length of fresh, unpeeled ginger root
- 4 tbsp sauce soy
- 6 nori sheets
- 3 tsp finely chopped crystallized ginger
- 3 green sliced onions scallions
- Eel Sauce Eel-Free if desired for dipping

NUTRITION

Calories 481 Kcal
Carbs 105 g | Fat 2 g
Protein 10 g

INSTRUCTIONS

1. Make your Butternut Squash Roll

2. Set aside around 12 strips of butternut, approximately 12 x 4 inches (1.25 x 10 cm) in length. Garlic & sliced ginger root should be added to the Vegetarian dashi in a small saucepan. Over high heat, quickly bring to a boil.

3. Add soy sauce and bring to a boil. Place the squash in a strainer or wire basket and bring it to a simmer in a pot of water.

4. Simmer the squash for 5-7 mins, or until it is tender but not mushy. Let everything cool fully after removing it from the boiling liquid.

5. Lay a rolling bamboo mat horizontally and place a nori sheet facing the rough side. Spread 12 cups (100g) of cooked sushi rice evenly on the bottom three-quarters of the nori.

6. Two butternut squash slices should be placed horizontally within the rice in the middle. You may have a little overlap in the middle if you want to.

7. Sprinkle the top with half a tsp of crystallized ginger. Add a few green onions to the mix.

VEGETARIAN

8. Once again, put your fingers in the water. Under a bamboo rolling pad, place your thumbs. Butternut squash should fit snugly on a folded piece of sushi mat. Make sure the folds don't trap the mat's edge!

9. Assist yourself to the mat's edge by lifting it. It's best if the nori stays put. Keep rolling until your roll is complete by placing your forefingers over the mat and your thumbs & middle fingers in the sides; gently form the roll.

10. On a cutting board, place the roll seam down. While you're waiting, go through the process again for the leftover rolls. Cut every roll into six equal pieces using a sharp knife soaked in water. Serve right away.

VEGAN SUSHI BOWLS

Prep Time — **15 MIN**
Cooking Time — **30 MIN**
Servings — **4**

INGREDIENTS

- 1 batch cashew mayo spicy
- 2 cups brown rice or cooked white
- 2 cups shelled edamame cooked
- 2 cups sweet potato peeled & cubed
- 1 cup grated carrot or julienned
- 1 cup cucumber diced
- 1 diced ripe avocado
- 8 tbsp nori sheets crumbled, or snacks roasted seaweed
- 4 tbsp seeds sesame
- green onion finely chopped
- soy sauce dash

INSTRUCTIONS

1. Blend all your ingredients unless smooth & creamy to produce the spicy vegan mayo. Learn how to make spicy mayonnaise here.

2. The sweet potato should be peeled and sliced into cubes, then boiled or steamed until fork soft. The rice & edamame should be cooked.

3. Carrots, cucumbers, and avocados should be sliced or julienned.

4. Once the rice has been added, add the remainder of the ingredients to the bowls one at a time.

5. Serve with a sprinkling of sesame seeds & a drizzle of soy sauce, if you choose.

NUTRITION

Calories 463 Kcal
Carbs 63 g | Fat 19 g
Protein 14 g

BROWN RICE QUINOA SUSHI ROLLS

- Prep Time — **40 MIN**
- Cooking Time — **45 MIN**
- Servings — **2**

INGREDIENTS

- 2/3 cup brown rice short grain
- 2 & 1/3 cups of water
- 1 sea salt pinch
- 2 tbsp vinegar rice
- 1 tbsp vinegar cider
- 1 tbsp of mirin
- 2 tbsp sugar turbinado
- ½ tsp salt sea
- ½ cup of quinoa
- 4 dry seaweed sheets nori
- ½ shredded carrot
- ½ cut in thin strips of cucumber
- 1 peeled, pitted, & cut into thin strips avocado

INSTRUCTIONS

1. Rinse & drain brown rice, then add water & sea salt to a pot & bring to a boil. Simmer the rice for around 30 mins on low heat with a lid on the pan. In the end, rice will not get mushy or shriveled.

2. When salt and sugar have dissolved in a bowl of vinegar (cider, mirin, rice, and sugar), add a pinch of sea salt. Set aside your vinegar mixture for later.

3. Mix rice and quinoa, bring to a boil, and decrease the heat to low; simmer until rice & quinoa are soft, and the liquid is absorbed for approximately 15 more mins. Pour the vinegar mixture over the rice and quinoa and gently stir to combine. Spread your grains as you stir to help grains dry & chill. Around 10 mins of fanning and stirring should do the trick.

4. Set a sushi mat on top of a sheet of nori. Using moist fingertips, apply a thin, equal coating of ¼ of rice mix to a nori sheet, leaving ½" of sheet exposed at its uppermost point. Shred some carrots, cucumber, and avocado into a line across the bottom of each serving.

5. Begin by picking up one of the rolling bamboo sheets and folding it up to enclose the sushi's contents. Then roll it up into a long, thick tube. It is necessary to carefully compress tightly compacted sushi once the roll is wrapped in a mat. Repeat this process with the leftover ingredients to create four more rolls.

NUTRITION

Calories 316 Kcal
Carbs 51 g | Fat 9 g
Protein 7 g

VEGETARIAN

CAULIFLOWER RICE SUSHI BOWLS

- Prep Time — **20 MIN**
- Cooking Time — **0 MIN**
- Servings — **2 BOWLS**

INGREDIENTS

For your cauliflower rice

- 16-oz bag of frozen complete thawed riced cauliflower
- 2 tbsp mild vinegar or rice vinegar
- 1 tsp of natural agave nectar or granulated sugar
- salt Pinch
- 6 seaweed snack pieces nori

Toppings

- Pitted avocado peeled & finely diced
- Kirby cucumber Thinly sliced
- carrots pre-grated
- nori thinly sliced seaweed snack
- optional Sesame seeds
- optional Pickled ginger
- to taste tamari or Soy sauce

NUTRITION

Calories 528 Kcal
Carbs 58 g | Fat 13 g
Protein 10 g

INSTRUCTIONS

1. Combine your cauliflower rice in vinegar, sugar, and salt in a mixing dish.
2. Cut your nori into long, thin strips with kitchen scissors and add cauliflower rice.
3. Divide your cauliflower rice mix into two dishes and serve each with a spoon. Place your toppings on top; there is no need to measure; just arrange what you think would look best.
4. If you want to use sesame seeds and ginger, add some extra seaweed snacks to the veggies.
5. Serve immediately with a dash of tamari or soy sauce to taste.

VARIATIONS

6. Any of the following may be used in place of the indicated toppings:
7. 3-4 finely cut shiitake mushroom tops
8. a few 2-inch-long spears of thin asparagus, gently steamed grated Turnip and daikon radish.

CAULIFLOWER RICE SUSHI BOWLS WITH TOFU

- Prep Time — **20 MIN**
- Cooking Time — **7 MIN**
- Servings — **4**

INGREDIENTS

For your dressing:

- ¼ cup neutral-flavored oil or canola oil
- 2 tsp soy sauce or tamari
- 2 tsp vinegar rice
- 1 tsp oil sesame
- 1 tsp syrup maple
- ¼ tsp optional sesame seeds

For your sushi bowls:

- 1 large cut in large chunks head cauliflower
- 1 tsp oil olive
- 1 6 oz thinly sliced baked tofu package
- 1 large thinly sliced cucumber spiralized
- 2 beets grated or spiralized small
- 2 avocados sliced in medium
- 1 cup nori chopped

INSTRUCTIONS

1. Make the dressing first. The dressing ingredients should be put in a small bowl and whisked until smooth.

2. The next step is to prepare the sushi. In your food processor, combine the cauliflower pieces and pulse until they are finely diced and rice-like in texture, approximately one min.

3. A medium-sized pan should be heated to medium-high heat & olive oil should be added. Cauliflower should be added to the oil when it is heated. Cook for 5 to 7 mins, tossing with a spatula as needed until your cauliflower is tender.

4. Divide your cauliflower rice into four equal bowls for sushi bowls. Assemble your bowls and garnish with an equal amount of avocado, tofu, cucumber, & nori (seaweed). The dressing may be added in any quantity to taste. Serve.

NUTRITION

Calories 460 Kcal
Carbs 26 g | Fat 36 g
Protein 15 g

VEGETARIAN

CHICKPEA SALAD SUSHI WRAP

- Prep Time — **25 MIN**
- Cooking Time — **0 MIN**
- Servings — **3**

INGREDIENTS

Rice:

- 2 cups of cooked rice short-grain
- 2 tbsp vinegar rice
- ¼ tsp of salt
- ¼ tsp of sugar

Chickpea Salad:

- ¾ cup of chickpeas
- ½ tsp granules of kelp
- ½ tsp powder onion
- ½ tsp powder garlic
- ½ tbsp mayo vegan
- ½ tbsp mustard Dijon
- salt & pepper Pinch

INSTRUCTIONS

1. Combine rice vinegar, rice, and a sprinkle of salt & sugar in a medium mixing dish. Make a well-balanced mixture and put it aside.
2. Chickpeas should be drained and rinsed, then mashed with a fork in a bowl.
3. A vegan mayo & Dijon mustard are excellent additions to the vegan mayo. As required, season with salt and pepper.
4. One nori sheet should be divided into two halves.
5. The last 2 quadrants should be filled with rice. Using wet fingertips, evenly distribute the rice and gently compress it down.
6. Add carrots to the final quadrant of the rice.
7. Add the chickpea salad to the 2nd quadrant & avocado slices to the 1st quadrant of the plate.
8. Optional: Put a little coconut aminos or soy sauce on one of the four corners. If you want, you may slather your wrap with soy sauce as you eat!
9. Fold the wrap over itself from the 1st-4th quadrant to produce a smaller square.
10. Enjoy! It's up to you whether you want to take it with you!

NUTRITION

Calories 440 Kcal
Carbs 60 g | Fat 16 g
Protein 18 g

CRISPY TOFU SUSHI BURRITO

Prep Time — **20 MIN**
Cooking Time — **15 MIN**
Servings — **3**

INGREDIENTS

Sushi Rice
- 1 cup rice sushi
- 3 tbsp vinegar rice
- 1 tbsp caster sugar raw
- ½ tsp salt sea

Crispy Tofu
- 250 grams tofu firm
- 3 tbsp corn starch or potato
- ½ tsp salt sea
- ¼ tsp pepper cayenne

Sushi Burrito
- 6 sheets nori
- ¼ cup mayonnaise chipotle
- ½ peeled & sliced avocado
- ½ cup carrots matchstick
- ½ cup kimchi vegan
- ½ cup spinach baby
- 1 tbsp pickled ginger

NUTRITION

Calories 544 Kcal
Carbs 70 g | Fat 23 g
Protein 13 g

INSTRUCTIONS

1. Rinse the sushi rice well until it is free of any sediment. At least five times a day, I wash and rinse my hair.

2. Add 1 and 14 cups of cold water to a medium pot with a cover, and add the rinsed rice. Bring the water to a boil over low to medium heat before lowering the heat, putting on the saucepan cover, and simmering the water until it is completely cooled. Remove the rice from the heat and let it in the pot with the cover on for 15 mins after the water has absorbed.

3. Meanwhile, whisk the vinegar, sugar, and salt in a separate bowl until the salt and sugar are completely dissolved.

4. After 15 mins, use a wooden spoon to gently stir the vinegar mixture into the rice in the glass or wooden bowl. Set the rice aside in a clean towel to cool it down to room temperature.

5. To remove as much moisture as possible, cover the tofu in a kitchen towel and let it rest for 5 mins. After that, cut the tofu into 2-inch cubes and store them in an airtight container.

6. Tofu should be coated on both sides with a mixture of corn starch, salt, and cayenne pepper, which may be found on a small plate.

7. Add the sunflower oil to a big pan and bring it to a boil. Fry each block of tofu for 2 mins on each side, or until it's crispy, to remove any extra starch. Tofu should be placed on an absorbent cloth after cooking.

VEGETARIAN

8. Assemble the burrito by soaking the short edges of two nori sheets and pushing them together with a rough surface. We want to make nori that is as long as possible.

9. Press your sushi rice into the nori, starting one inch from the edge until it is as even as possible. Rice should be pressed into a square 3" long & the same breadth as a nori sheet to make the desired shape. Chipotle mayonnaise, baby spinach, crispy tofu block, matchstick carrots, avocado slices, kimchi, & pickled ginger are all great additions to this dish.

10. Gently roll your nori out from you, starting at the edge nearest to you. Just roll it over and over again, and you'll get rid of any imperfections in the nori. Use cold water to seal the nori roll by running a line along the edge. Seal the roll by laying it seam-side-down for a few seconds. Serve the tortilla by slicing it in half.

STIR FRY NOODLES WITH SHRIMPS

Prep Time — **20 MIN**
Cooking Time — **20 MIN**
Servings — **4**

INGREDIENTS

- 1 Cup and 2 Tbs water
- ¾ Teaspoon granulated sugar
- 1 ½ Teaspoons salt
- 3 Cups bread flour
- 2 Tablespoons wheat germ
- 1 ¾ active dry yeast
- Cornmeal

INSTRUCTIONS

1. Add water, sugar, salt, bread flour, wheat germ and yeast to the bread pan. Place the bread pan into the bread machine. Press "prog". Choose "dough program". Press "start".

2. After the cycle has been complete, take the dough out of the machine & transfer to your kitchen table. Cover with plastic & rest for 10 minutes.

3. Divide it into 2 portions. Form a baguette from the 2 portions. Dust your baking pan with cornmeal. Place the baguette on top of the baking pan. Cover with plastic.

NUTRITION

Calories 354 Kcal
Carbs 11 g | Fat 21 g | Protein 35 g

VEGAN SUSHI BURRITO W/ AIR FRYER TOFU

Prep Time — **30 MIN**
Cooking Time — **25 MIN**
Servings — **2**

INGREDIENTS

- ¼ block pressed & sliced tofu extra firm
- 1 tbsp soy sauce low-sodium
- ¼ tsp ginger ground
- ¼ tsp powder garlic
- to taste sriracha sauce
- 2 cups of Pressure Cooker cooked & cooled Sushi Rice
- 2 nori sheets

Filling Ingredients

- tofu
- ¼ sliced into thin pieces Hass avocado
- 3 tbsp mango sliced
- 1 just green parts green onion
- 2 tbsp optional pickled ginger
- 2 tbsp breadcrumbs panko

NUTRITION

Calories 364 Kcal
Carbs 90 g | Fat 6 g
Protein 11 g

INSTRUCTIONS

MAKE YOUR AIR FRYER TOFU

1. Combine the ginger, garlic, soy sauce, & sriracha sauce in a small bowl. Toss the tofu in the marinade until it is well-coated. Wait for ten mins and then pick up where you left off.

2. Transfer your tofu to the air fryer basket & cook for around 15 mins at 370 deg F, shaking every 8 mins for the first 15 mins.

MAKE THE SUSHI BURRITO

3. Cover your nori with sushi rice, leaving approximately 12 inches of space around the nori, "a sliver of nori on one side. To avoid sticking, use moistened fingers.

4. About half of a centimeter "Place half of each filling ingredient, except for the panko, on the rice, starting from the nori sheet's covered edge, as shown in the video. Sprinkle 1 tbsp of breadcrumbs on these of the fillings.

5. You'll seal the sushi burrito with the exposed portion of nori by rolling the sushi burrito across once. Before serving, let your roll stand with the closed side down for five mins.

6. Re-create your sushi burrito by using the second nori sheet & the rest of the ingredients.

VEGETARIAN

FURIKAKE SUSHI CASSEROLE

Prep Time — **15 MIN**
Cooking Time — **50 MIN**
Servings — **6**

INGREDIENTS

- 2 cups rice sushi
- 1-2 tbsp rice vinegar seasoned
- 2 large avocados Hass
- 1 medium shredded carrot
- 2 small cucumbers Persian
- ¼ cup furikake
- 1 glass dish baking

Homemade Furikake

- 2 sheets of seaweed toasted nori
- ¼ cup toasted sesame seeds white & black
- 1 tsp salt coarse
- 1 tsp sugar coconut

NUTRITION

Calories 294 Kcal
Carbs 49 g | Fat 5 g
Protein 2 g

INSTRUCTIONS

1. Rinse the rice thoroughly until you see clear water. Let it soak for 30 mins, then cook it in a saucepan, add the correct quantity of water according to the packing instructions and start cooking it. Bring it to a boil on the burner.

2. Cover your pot using a lid & turn the heat down to a low simmer after it reaches a boil. Remove and add a little water if needed.

3. Ten minutes after removing the pot from the heat, return it to the stove and cook for another 20 minutes, to eliminate all water or until soft but with a little texture. Uncover & fluff using a fork when it has been set.

4. Once rice has cooled, add vinegar to the mixture and taste.

5. Place furikake on top of the rice within the baking dish before baking.

6. Sliced cucumbers and julienned carrots should be layered on top of each other. Finally, garnish the dish with avocado, if desired. Rather than slicing the avocado into cubes, we like to scoop all of the avocados into a casserole dish and then spread it out evenly with a spatula.

7. To finish, top with the leftover furikake, to taste.

8. You can serve your sushi casserole like lasagna by cutting it into squares and garnishing it with nori. Use your hands to scoop a portion of the casserole into the nori sheet, then dive in with pleasure!

EGGPLANT SUSHI

🍙 Prep Time — **45 MIN**
🍜 Cooking Time — **30 MIN**
🍴 Servings — **4-5**

INGREDIENTS

Sushi

- 4 to 5 sheets of nori
- 2 cups of rice sushi
- 3 tbsp vinegar rice
- 1 tbsp sugar or maple syrup
- ½ tsp sea salt fine

Filling

- 2 tbsp seeds sesame
- 1 & ½ tsp sesame oil toasted
- 2 tbsp soy sauce or tamari (for a Gluten Free version)
- 1 tbsp syrup maple
- 4 tsp vinegar rice
- ½ tsp chili sauce spicy
- 2 aubergines / small eggplants
- 1 oz leaves baby spinach
- 1 peeled & julienned carrot
- 1 cored & julienned Lebanese cucumber

Condiments

- wasabi
- soy sauce or tamari
- pickled ginger, homemade or store-bought

INSTRUCTIONS

SUSHI RICE

1. Sushi rice should be thoroughly rinsed until the water is clear. A glass bowl makes it easy to see whether the food has been thoroughly cleaned.

2. Add water to the washed rice inside a medium saucepan with a glass top. Bring the mixture to a boil by covering it with a lid. Allow rice to simmer until all water has been absorbed, then turn down the heat to low & let your rice rest for a few mins before serving (around 10 mins). Then, turn off the heat but don't remove the lid, & let your covered pot stay on a warm stove for the next 5 to 10 mins so that the food may finish cooking naturally.

3. Mix maple syrup (sugar), rice vinegar, & salt in a separate bowl while your rice is cooking. Adjust the sweetness & saltiness to suit your palate.

4. Season the cooked rice with the mixture you produced earlier by gently mixing the seasonings into your rice using a spatula on a wide baking sheet. You can speed up the rice's cooling process by fanning it if you've got the time.

NUTRITION

Calories 390 Kcal
Carbs 11 g | Fat 5 g
Protein 10 g

VEGETARIAN

FILLING

5. Toast your sesame seeds in a hot pan for a few mins until they're brown and aromatic. Use a mortar and pestle to break them up into smaller pieces.

6. In a small bowl, combine sesame oil, rice vinegar, maple syrup, tamari (soy sauce), and sambal oelek. Set the sesame seeds away & add the crushed sesame seeds.

7. Cut the eggplants into 112 cm / 0.5" long slices using a sharp knife. If you typically do this, salt your eggplant slices from both sides & let them for around 60 mins to bring out any bitterness that may have been there. To remove the salt from the slices, just rinse them in water and pat them dry.

8. Set a griddle pan to medium-high heat and prepare your food. When the pan is heated, coat it with olive oil & then add the slices of eggplant. Approximately 5 mins from each side are enough time to cook until soft.

9. Turn down the heat & let your slices cool. Take three long strips from each piece of meat (lengthwise), bathe them in the marinade, and then serve with your favorite dipping sauce.

10. A tiny bowl of rice vinegar mixed with maple syrup (sugar) & salt. Adjust the sweetness & saltiness to the preference.

11. Gently stir the spice into your rice using a spatula to transfer the rice to a big tray (a wide Pyrex works nicely). It's a good idea to wait until the rice has cooled down before fanning it if you do have enough time.

ASSEMBLY

12. Cover your sushi mat (wrapped kitchen towel or bamboo mat) & have a medium bowl full of water nearby. A nori sheet is placed shiny side right over the mat. Assemble your sushi by evenly spreading out the nori sheet with some chilled sushi rice, leaving a 2 cm margin at the top to seal. In addition to distributing the rice evenly, use the back of a spoon to push it into the mat.

13. Arrange long strands of chopped fresh spinach, cucumber matchsticks & eggplant slices on one side of a nori sheet and allow some room below to fold your nori sheet on the filling later on.

14. Squeezing the roll firmly using your hands while gently rolling it on the mat is good. Check-in on the project from time to time to ensure that everything is in place and secure.

15. The next step is to brush water on the edge of the roll with your finger to seal it. Set your roll aside after you're done rolling. Repeat the previous four procedures with the rest of the nori sheets.

16. Using the sharp knife, slice all sushi rolls into 1cm pieces. Serve with tamari, wasabi, & ginger pickles (soy sauce).

HOMEMADE VEGAN SUSHI ROLLS W/ QUINOA STICKY RICE

Prep Time — **20 MIN**
Cooking Time — **20 MIN**
Servings — **4**

INGREDIENTS

- ½ cup sushi rice uncooked
- ½ cup quinoa dry
- 2 cups of broth or water
- 2 Tbsp vinegar rice
- 1/8 to ¼ tsp sugar
- 1/8 to ¼ tsp salt
- 4 nori sheets
- 10 blanched asparagus spears
- ¼ to ½ cucumber English
- 1 to 2 carrots large
- ½ bell pepper large yellow
- 4 to 8 onions green
- to taste broccoli/clover sprouts
- for topping sesame seeds & chia seeds toasted

INSTRUCTIONS

1. Put a small saucepan on medium-high heat
2. Rinse the quinoa well. Drain it, then put in the saucepan, frequently stirring while you gently toast it for an additional nutty taste.
3. Turn up the heat to the highest setting and add the rice and two cups of water.
4. Cover & simmer on medium heat for 20 mins, until it reaches boiling point. Add vinegar, salt and sugar to the hot and foamy mixture, after 5 minutes or when cooled down a bit.
5. Split the fluffiness into 2 separate bowls to chill.
6. While rice & quinoa simmer, prepare vegetables: To make asparagus softer, trim the ends and blanch them for a short time in hot water. Cut your bell pepper & cucumber into small slices, julienne your carrots next. With your green onion snippers at the ready, gather a large handful of sprouts and many strips.
7. Place a nori sheet on top of a plastic-wrapped bamboo mat.
8. Spread the quinoa & rice inside a uniform layer on the seaweed sheet using a big spoon. The vegetables should be arranged in three rows at the end of the page.
9. Fish and cream cheese may also be added here if desired. Slice, roll, then spread sesame seeds on top of the rolls!

NUTRITION

Calories 191 Kcal
Carbs 38 g | Fat 9 g
Protein 6 g

VEGETARIAN

MANGO SUSHI BOWL

- Prep Time — **20 MIN**
- Cooking Time — **0 MIN**
- Servings — **4**

INGREDIENTS

- For the pickled vegetables:
- 1 carrot large peeled & trimmed into ribbon
- 1 cucumber large peeled & trimmed into ribbon
- 1 & ¼ cups of water warm
- 1 & ¼ cups of Nakano Rice Vinegar Mango Seasoned
- 1 tbsp nectar agave
- ½ tsp of salt
- For the sushi bowl:
- 2 cups of cooked rice brown
- 2 tbsp of Nakano Mango Rice Vinegar Seasoned
- 1 tbsp of tamari
- ½ tsp of salt
- 1 cup mango cubed
- 1 cup cooked edamame shelled
- 2 scallions white & light green thinly sliced parts
- ½ tsp seeds sesame

INSTRUCTIONS

MAKE THE QUICK-PICKLED VEGETABLES:

1. Split into two containers with re-sealable lids and add the carrot & cucumber strips. To make a dressing: Combine the nectar, salt, vinegar, agave, and pepper in a small dish and mix well.

2. Divide the mixture equally between the 2 containers and pour it over the veggie ribbons. Shake the containers a few times before putting them away. After that, refrigerate the containers for one hr in the refrigerator. A longer period in the freezer is OK.

3. In the meanwhile, prepare the brown rice. Combine your tamari, rice vinegar, & salt in a mixing bowl. In a separate bowl, whisk the other ingredients together until smooth. Drizzle over the hot rice and gently mix. Set away for later.

ASSEMBLE SUSHI BOWLS:

4. Make four equal servings of rice. Add the edamame, mango, & scallions, and part of the quick-pickled veggies. Sesame seeds may be sprinkled on top. Serve right away.

NUTRITION

Calories 476 Kcal
Carbs 92 g | Fat 5 g
Protein 13 g

QUINOA SUSHI ROLLS W/ MISO-SESAME DIPPING SAUCE

- Prep Time — **20 MIN**
- Cooking Time — **20 MIN**
- Servings — **3 ROLLS**

- 2 tsp honey or agave syrup
- 1 tsp freshly grated ginger
- 1 tsp seeds sesame

INGREDIENTS

For the Quinoa Sushi Rolls:

- 1 cup rinsed well quinoa uncooked
- 1 & ½ cups of water
- ½ cup of vinegar rice
- 2 tsp honey or agave syrup
- 2 tsp of salt
- 3 Nori seaweed sheets
- 1 peeled & sliced avocado pitted
- ½ peeled & sliced into matchsticks cucumber large
- 1 peeled & grated beet medium
- ½ cup microgreens or sprouts

For the Miso-Sesame Sauce:

- 2 tbsp miso white
- 1 tbsp Juice of one lime

INSTRUCTIONS

1. Set a medium pot over high heat, then add your quinoa & water. Add water and bring to a boil, then reduce the heat & cover. Simmer for 15 to 20 mins, till your quinoa is cooked and still a little undercooked. The quinoa will have absorbed the water, but it will still be cloudy.

2. Meanwhile, cook the honey, rice vinegar, and salt in a medium saucepan. Simmer just long enough for the quinoa to cook, then turn off the heat and let it rest.

3. In a saucepan, combine the vinegar mixture with your quinoa, mix well, cover, & let rest for at least an hr till the quinoa has absorbed the liquid. Allow the quinoa to cool fully after removing it from the heat.

4. Mix up your Dipping Miso-Sesame Sauce while your quinoa cools. Add the sauce ingredients to a medium bowl and mix well. Take a sip and see whether you need to add more honey. Serve chilled, if possible.

5. Put a plastic wrap over the top of a bamboo mat & begin rolling the sushi. Use plastic wrap to cover a Nori strip. Cover the Nori with 1/3 of the quinoa, leaving a little border around the edges. The beets, avocado, cucumber, and sprouts (microgreens) should all be placed in the middle of the quinoa, with the other ingredients being placed around it.

NUTRITION

Calories 410 Kcal
Carbs 59 g | Fat 9 g
Protein 14 g

6. To begin rolling, begin with the end closest to your body. Bring about the end up & roll firmly over the filling, pushing as you go, using a bamboo mat as a guide. Seal the edges by pressing them together.

7. Using a bowl of water, soak all edges of a Nori and try again if they don't seal well. Slice the sushi into six to eight pieces with a sharp knife. Dip inside the dipping sauce before serving. Refrigerated remains keep for two days when stored in an airtight container.

SUSHI BURRITO BOWL

Prep Time — **20 MIN**
Cooking Time — **0 MIN**
Servings — **2**

INGREDIENTS

- 1 diced sweet potato
- 1 tbsp oil olive
- pepper & Salt
- 1 to 2 peeled large carrots
- ½ to 1 cup cooked jasmine rice
- ½ cup thawed when frozen edamame
- ½ diced English cucumber
- 1 sliced avocado

NUTRITION

Calories 534 Kcal
Carbs 58 g | Fat 16 g | Protein 16 g

INSTRUCTIONS

1. The oven should be preheated at 425 degrees Fahrenheit.

2. Bake sweet potatoes by slicing them into cubes. Salt & pepper are added to the olive oil, and the mixture is mixed well to include them. The sweet potato should be baked for 15 to 20 minutes unless it's fork-tender.

3. Carrot strands may be made while your sweet potatoes are cooking with a vegetable peeler. Set away for later.

4. Assemble your dishes when your sweet potato is ready: Serve the rice in two separate dishes.

5. This dish is best served with vegan Sriracha mayonnaise, sesame seeds, seaweed, & sriracha sauce on top (if desired).

ROASTED SWEET POTATO SUSHI

Prep Time — **15 MIN**
Cooking Time — **30 MIN**
Servings — **3**

INGREDIENTS

For the Sweet Potato Filling

- 1 tbsp of oil vegetable
- 1 tbsp of syrup maple
- 1 tsp of oil sesame
- 1 sweet potato large

For the Rice

- 1 cup rice sushi
- 1 & 1/3 cups of water
- 1 & ½ tbsp vinegar rice
- ¾ tbsp of salt

For Rolling and Serving

- 3 nori sheets
- 2 large scallions
- sesame seeds toasted
- pickled ginger
- wasabi
- soy sauce

NUTRITION

Calories 456 Kcal
Carbs 86 g | Fat 7 g
Protein 8 g

INSTRUCTIONS

1. Set oven temperature to 375' F.
2. Combine olive oil, maple syrup, & sesame oil
3. Peel sweet potatoes & slice into strips ½" thick. Toss in oil & maple syrup mix to chicken before frying. On baking sheet, arrange strips in single layer. Bake for 25 mins.
4. Rinse rice in cold water for 1 mins.
5. Add water, vinegar, & salt to small pot & bring to boil. Place in hot oven. Squirts of water. Before serving, take it off the heat & simmer for 20 mins, or until liquid is absorbed. Before removing the lid, let it rest for around 10 mins.
6. You will need bamboo mat & small bowl of water to soak hands while working. Use the bamboo mat to place anyone sheets. Wet your hands and spread a thin coating of rice over the nori. Three-fifths of the sweet potato strips should be arranged in a single line across the nori's breadth, an inch from you. Assort your sweet potato slices with a few onion pieces.
7. Roll your fillings firmly with the bamboo mat & nori end nearest you. Continue rolling by tucking the tip of nori inside and pressing the roll with the mat to keep it in place. Slice the rolled pastry into eight equal pieces when finished rolling.
8. Repeat this process with the leftover nori sheets & fillings that you have.
9. Sesame seeds, wasabi, soy sauce, and pickled ginger are needed to accompany this dish.

SWEET POTATO TEMPURA & AVOCADO ROLLS W/ TERIYAKI GLAZE

- Prep Time — **30 MIN**
- Cooking Time — **15 MIN**
- Servings — **4**

INGREDIENTS

For Teriyaki Glaze

- 1 cup sugar brown
- 1 cup of mirin
- 1/8 cup of sake
- ½ cup sauce soy
- 1 Tbsp sesame oil toasted
- 1 Tbsp ginger minced

For Sushi Rice

- 1 cup rice sushi
- 1 cup of water
- 1 tsp vinegar rice
- 1 tsp sugar
- ½ tsp salt

For Sweet Potato Tempuras

- Vegetable, oil
- 1 peeled sweet potato
- 1 Tbsp Egg Vegan
- 1 & ¼ cup fizzy water ice-cold
- 1 cup flour AP
- 1 tsp salt

To Assemble & Finish

- 4 nori sheets toasted
- 4 Tbsp seeds sesame
- 1 sliced ripe avocado
- 2-4 Tbsp Vegenaise
- pickled ginger & wasabi

INSTRUCTIONS

FOR TERIYAKI GLAZE

1. Prepare an Asian-inspired dish by mixing all ingredients in a large bowl. Set away for a later time.

2. A small saucepan should be used to heat the toasted sesame oil. Add the ginger and coat it thoroughly with the oil before adding it. Only cook for a min at a time.

3. In a saucepan, add the bowl materials, stirring it at first to dissolve all sugar. Turn down the heat to the lowest level after reaching a tiny boil. Remove from heat and let decrease for 30 to 35 mins, whisking periodically.

4. To thicken your teriyaki sauce, chill it in the refrigerator. If it gets too thick, microwave it for a few seconds to slightly loosen it up.

NUTRITION

Calories 284 Kcal
Carbs 33 g | Fat 16 g
Protein 5 g

FOR SUSHI RICE

5. Cook the rice in a rice cooker with water & rice. Reserved to cool after adding the sugar, rice vinegar, & salt.

6. For Sweet Potato Tempuras

7. A small iron pot should be filled with several centimeters of oil to begin. Using medium-high heat, bring it to 350'. A few mins later, the oil would be ready for use. Insert the dry chopstick into heated oil and wait until it reaches the pot's base to see when it's done. You're ready to cook if bubbles develop around it right away.

8. Put together the VeganEgg and a bottle of very cold soda water.

9. Chopsticks may be used to mix in the flour. It is OK if there are some bumps in the road. The tempura will get thick if you overmix it.

10. Take caution while placing the potatoes into the oil since they burn quickly. Drain on paper towels while the remainder of the food is fried. While the oil is gleaming, add a little salt to taste.

TO ASSEMBLE & FINISH

11. Divide your cooled rice into four equal halves. A sushi mat may be slipped into a Ziploc bag or wrapped with plastic wrap. Place a nori sheet on the mat with the glossy side facing down. Spread your rice evenly on the nori sheet, allowing approximately an inch uncovered at the top, using your fingertips moistened with water. Add a spoonful of sesame seeds to the dish.

12. Place 2-3 pieces of potato tempura on the side nearest to you, with the uncovered end facing away from you. Avocado and mayonnaise are optional additions.

13. The sushi should be rolled away from you while maintaining a firm yet gentle grasp on the mat. Water or some rice grains may assist seal the end after being wrapped up and rolled.

14. After that, using a sharp knife, cut every sushi in half, then into halves, until you have eight equal pieces.

15. To produce another four rolls and arrange them on a serving platter, repeat the procedure. Serve with wasabi & pickled ginger, if preferred, on top of the teriyaki glaze.

VEGETARIAN

TOFU & MUSHROOM KIMBAP WRAP

Prep Time — 10 MIN
Cooking Time — 20 MIN
Servings — 2

INGREDIENTS

Rice:
- 2 cups rice short-grain
- 1 tsp oil sesame
- ¼ tsp salt

Pan-fried "Tofu Egg":
- 1 tsp of oil
- ¼ firm tofu block medium
- ¼ tsp of Kala Namak

Garlic Mushrooms:
- ½ tsp oil
- 1 cup of mushrooms
- ½ tsp powder garlic
- salt Pinch

INSTRUCTIONS

1. Slicing the tofu into cubes will make it easier to cook. Tofu should be cooked for 3 to 5 mins on all sides until golden brown in a skillet heated to medium-high heat.

2. Sprinkle every tofu piece with a little amount of black salt. Set away for a later time.

3. Cook the mushrooms by chopping them up and adding them to a skillet. Toss in some garlic salt. Set away for a later time.

4. One nori sheet should be divided into two halves.

5. The last 2 quadrants should be filled with rice. Using wet fingertips, evenly distribute the rice and gently compress it down.

6. Cooked mushrooms & shredded carrots go over one of the rice-filled quadrants.

7. In the first quadrant, place the spinach; in the second, the tofu.

8. Fold your wrap over itself from the first to the fourth quadrant to produce a smaller square. Enjoy!

NUTRITION

Calories 329 Kcal
Carbs 57 g | Fat 12 g
Protein 10 g

VEGAN SUSHI BOWL W/ SESAME SOY DRESSING

- Prep Time — **30 MIN**
- Cooking Time — **0 MIN**
- Servings — **4**

INGREDIENTS

Sushi bowls

- 1 peeled in strips medium carrot
- 1 thinly sliced cucumber
- 1 seeded & thinly sliced bell pepper
- 1 cubed avocado
- 1 cup thawed frozen edamame
- 1 cup Jasmine Rice cooked

Additional toppings

- sushi ginger pickled
- sesame seeds black
- optional roasted seaweed

Quick pickle sauce

- ½ cup of water
- ¼ tbsp vinegar rice
- salt pinch

sesame soy dressing

- 2 tbsp sauce soy
- 1 tbsp oil sesame
- 1 tbsp vinegar rice
- 1/8 tsp optional wasabi

INSTRUCTIONS

1. In a small bowl, combine your ingredients for a quick pickle sauce. Ensure the carrots and cucumbers are well soaked in the liquid before adding them. The remainder of your dinner may be prepared while the salad is chilling.

2. Rice should be cooked.

3. The avocado, bell pepper, & edamame should be ready to eat now.

4. Set aside your dressing ingredients for later use.

5. By splitting the rice into four separate bowls, you may assemble your bowls. Pickled veggies, red bell peppers, and edamame should be distributed evenly. Sesame seeds & pickled ginger provide a tasty finishing touch for this dish. Serve with Dressing right away.

NUTRITION

Calories 240 Kcal
Carbs 24 g | Fat 13 g
Protein 8 g

VEGETARIAN

VEGAN SUSHI SANDWICH

- Prep Time — **20 MIN**
- Cooking Time — **25 MIN**
- Servings — **4**

INGREDIENTS

- ½ firm tofu block
- 3 tbsp sauce soy
- 1 tbsp vinegar rice
- 4 whole sheets of nori
- 1 cup sushi rice cooked
- 1 grated carrot
- 8 lettuce leaves
- 1 tbsp sauce tamari

INSTRUCTIONS

1. Soy sauce & rice vinegar should be marinated for almost 1 hr before use.

2. Lay the nori sheet out on a level surface. To construct a square of the same dimension as the tofu, generously spoon in the sushi rice. Lettuce & then tofu should be added next.

3. Optionally, top with other ingredients of your choosing, then add a 2nd layer of rice, and press down firmly. Fold the nori sheet in half, keeping the filling in place. Assemble the opposite side by tucking the sides in and folding it over.

4. Slice using the sharp knife after flipping it over to the other side and serve with some tamari sauce. Enjoy your sandwich!

NUTRITION

Calories 105 Kcal
Carbs 13 g | Fat 2 g
Protein 8 g

DESSERTS & SPECIALS

FRUIT SUSHI RICE

- Prep Time — **20 MIN**
- Cooking Time — **15 MIN**
- Servings — **6**

INGREDIENTS

- 2 cups Grain Rice Short
- ½ cup milk coconut
- 2 tbsp sugar granulated
- 1 tsp extract vanilla
- 1 lb hulled & sliced strawberries
- 2 peeled & sliced kiwis
- ½ can of drained mandarin oranges
- 4 tsp black & white toasted sesame seeds
- 1 tbsp lime zest grated

INSTRUCTIONS

1. Prepare and cook the rice. Gently stir in the coconut milk, sugar, and vanilla with a rubber spatula. Allow for complete cooling.

2. Place an 11-by-10-inch rectangle of clingfilm on a work surface, then place a 9 x 8-inch plastic wrap on the work surface and spread the rice in the center, pressing the rice into an even layer with your fingertips.

3. Lay the fruit over the rice in a straight line, beginning 1" from one edge. If you're using plastic wrap, start rolling it tighter over the filling and then continue to form a roll. Finish up with the rest of the grains and fruits.

4. After removing the plastic wrap, cut the rolls into 2" pieces. Remove the wrap. Make a garnish of lime zest & sesame seeds. These fruit sushi rolls, a playful reinterpretation of a traditional Japanese dish, are a delight for the whole family!

NUTRITION

Calories 204 Kcal
Carbs 12 g | Fat 20 g
Protein 21 g

DESSERTS & SPECIALS

FIG & COCONUT DESSERT SUSHI

Prep Time — **35 MIN**
Cooking Time — **25 MIN**
Servings — **2**

INGREDIENTS

- ½ cup shredded coconut unsweetened
- ½ cup cream coconut
- 1 large sliced black or brown fig
- ¼ teaspoon extract vanilla
- ¼ teaspoon salt high-quality
- 1-2 tablespoons of maple syrup or honey
- 2 tortilla wraps (paleo suggested)

Sweet "wasabi"

- 2 chopped green small figs

Apple "ginger" slices

- ½ a sliced peeled apple
- half lemon Juice

Lime finger "fish eggs", optional

- 1 lime finger

NUTRITION

Calories 284 Kcal
Carbs 20 g | Fat 19 g
Protein 25 g

INSTRUCTIONS

1. To make things simpler, lay down a parchment paper, sushi mat, or plastic wrap. Wrap it in a pure wrapper.

2. Coconut cream & shredded coconut can be mixed in a bowl. You can also use maple syrup or honey as a sweetener if desired. Forks are ideal for combining components.

3. Leave 1" around the corners of the paleo wrap and spread the coconut mix in the square. Fork-mashed the mixture uniformly and spread it out on a baking sheet.

4. Set aside some of your figs to garnish the upper half of your wrap.

5. Roll the sushi like you would a tiny carpet, beginning with the edge, which has figs over it.

6. Slice it into small rounds after being rolled up with a very sharp knife. You should be able to slice eight equal pieces.

7. Cut an apple in half and slice it very thinly. For best result you can use a mandolin. Apple slices should be drizzled with lemon juice to prevent browning before being placed beside your sushi roll.

8. To make the sweet version of "wasabi," puree 1-2 green figs inside a food processor. Place it next to sushi on the plate.

9. Squeeze the juice from a finger lime if you have one. Add a little lime "caviar" on the top of every piece of sushi. You're all set to surprise your sushi-loving buddies and yourself with your culinary prowess!

SWEET SUSHI WITH CHOCOLATE

- Prep Time — **45 MIN**
- Cooking Time — **5 H 30 MIN**
- Servings — **4**

INGREDIENTS

For the chocolate coating

- 200 milliliters cream whipped
- 250 grams couverture dark
- 200 grams couverture milk chocolate
- 2 centiliters cognac
- 100 grams butter soft

For rice

- 500 milliliters milk coconut
- 150 grams sugar
- 250 grams rice arborio
- 200 grams ripe strawberries fresh

INSTRUCTIONS

1. In a dish, break up the couverture chocolate into small pieces. Bring the cream to a boil, then add your chocolate chunks and whisk until smooth. Gradually incorporate the cognac. Add the butter gradually to the chocolate cream by slicing it into little pieces.

2. Let the chocolate cream cool for at least five hours on a parchment-lined baking sheet. Bring the coconut milk and sugar to a boil in a separate saucepan before stirring in the rice. Stirring every few minutes, simmer for approximately 30 minutes at a medium-low temperature. Strawberry stems should be trimmed, and the fruit should be sliced after it has been rinsed.

3. Over the chocolate, evenly spread the chilled rice pudding. Sliced strawberries should be placed in the middle. You should be able to form a 3cm thick roll. Serve with thick pieces cut off the board.

NUTRITION

Calories 320 Kcal
Carbs 15 g | Fat 25 g
Protein 40 g

DESSERTS & SPECIALS

SWEET SUSHI W/ KIWI RHUBARB

- Prep Time — **50 MIN**
- Cooking Time — **35 MIN**
- Servings — **4**

INGREDIENTS

- 1 lemongrass sprig
- 2 ginger centimeters
- 200 sarborio rice gram
- 400 milliliters can milk coconut
- 50 grams sugar palm
- 2-star anise
- 1 rhubarb large
- 6 kiwis
- 1 juiced lime
- 2 tbsp sugar powdered
- 1 tbsp of sugar

INSTRUCTIONS

1. Lemongrass should be trimmed and rinsed. Cucumber should be peeled and sliced. Cook the rice, palm sugar, coconut milk, and star anise in a mixture for 15 to 20 minutes on the stovetop at a low temperature. Take a kitchen towel, cover the rice, and let it sit for around 25-30 minutes until your rice is soft and the liquid has evaporated. Allow the rice to chill for 40 minutes in the refrigerator.

2. Rhubarb may be prepared by peeling it, then cutting it in half crosswise. Use a vegetable peeler to make thin slices cut lengthwise. Rhubarb slices are added to boiling water along with the granulated sugar. Drain on paper towels for a few minutes before serving.

3. Set aside two kiwis for later. Combine the powdered sugar with the leftover kiwis & mash until smooth. Add lime juice and press through a filter into a small basin.

4. Shape the rice into oval rolls using the palm for sushi. Cut the kiwis into thin wedges by slicing them lengthwise. Wrap each roll with a rhubarb slice and top with a kiwi wedge. Japanese-style plates should be used to serve two sushi rolls. Serve with a small cup of kiwi sauce.

NUTRITION

Calories 354 Kcal
Carbs 16 g | Fat 24 g
Protein 32 g

KEY LIME DESSERT SUSHI

- Prep Time — **20 MIN**
- Cooking Time — **4 H 20 MIN**
- Servings — **4**

INGREDIENTS

Cake

- 2/3 cup of Gold Medal all-purpose flour unbleached
- 1 teaspoon powder baking
- ¼ teaspoon salt
- ½ cup sugar granulated
- 3 eggs
- 1 teaspoon vanilla extract pure
- 2 tablespoons sugar powdered

Filling

- 1 cup sugar granulated
- 3 tablespoons all-purpose flour unbleached
- 1 egg, beaten lightly
- ¾ cup of water
- ¼ cup juice key lime
- for garnish, Whipped cream
- 1 for garnish lime, sliced

NUTRITION

Calories 124 Kcal
Carbs 9 g | Fat 10 g
Protein 25 g

INSTRUCTIONS

1. Preheat your oven to 375°F. You may use a cooking spray & parchment paper to line a rimmed baking sheet. Set the paper or mat aside to be coated with extra frying spray.

2. Combine flour, baking powder, and salt in a small bowl, then mix well.

3. Beat the eggs, sugar, & egg whites over high speed in a medium basin or the bowl of a stand mixer until they are pale and fluffy, approximately 5 minutes. Add a dash of vanilla.

4. Stir in the flour mixture into two batches until it is completely combined.

5. Spread the batter with a spatula once poured onto the cookie sheet. Bake for 10 minutes till a light touch causes the cake to bounce back.

6. Toss a big tea towel in the powdered sugar while the cake is baking. Once it's out of the oven, gently flip it onto the tea towel. Take off the parchment paper or silicone mat before cutting the cake. Prepare a tea towel and set it on the seam side down on the countertop for 30-60 minutes to allow the cakes to cool.

7. While you're doing so, prepare the filling: Sugar, flour, egg, water, and key lime juice are all mixed in a small pot; when the mix comes to a boil, cook & stir for 1 minute more until thick. Cool to ambient temp after straining through a cloth into a different bowl.

8. A layer of plastic wrap should be placed over each cake after cooling. Roll each cake firmly

DESSERTS & SPECIALS

after spreading half of the filling on top. Place the two cakes in the refrigerator for at least four hours or overnight to cool and harden.

9. Using a knife, cut the plastic wrap off the cakes that have been refrigerated and frozen. Make 1 inch slices out of each cake using a sharp knife. Top with a lime slice and whipped cream, then flip over to the cut-side-down position. If preferred, serve with a dipping sauce of heated chocolate.

COCKTAIL SUSHI

Prep Time — **60 MIN**
Cooking Time — **30 MIN**
Servings — **12**

INGREDIENTS

- 1 standard quantity Sushi Rice

Tuna Collins

- 1 1/2 oz (40 g) fresh tuna, cut into small dice
- 1 teaspoon soy sauce
- 1/2 avocado, cut into small pieces
- A few broccoli sprouts or kaiware daikon sprouts for garnish

Egg Nog

- 1 egg
- 1 tablespoon sugar
- Dash of Salt
- 1 teaspoon mirin
- 4 sprigs of chervil or parsley for garnish

Cheese-Mopolitan

- 1/3 Japanese cucumber, finely diced (30 g)
- 1 oz (30 g) tomatoes, finely diced
- 1 oz (30 g) Monterey Jack or other natural cheese, finely diced

INSTRUCTIONS

1. Prepare the Sushi Rice. Divide it into 3 portions.

2. To make the Tuna Collins sushi, marinate the diced tuna in the soy sauce for 5 minutes. Add the tuna and the avocado to one portion of the Basic Sushi Rice. Mix gently and divide the rice among four cocktail glasses (or other serving dishes). Garnish with the sprouts, and cut them into small lengths.

3. To make the Egg Nog sushi, mix the egg, sugar, salt and mirin in a microwave-safe bowl. Microwave for 1 minute and mix well with a fork.

NUTRITION

Calories 238 Kcal
Carbs 31 g | Fat 2 g
Protein 12 g

4. Microwave once again for another 30 seconds and mix once again, this time thoroughly with a fork, to make a very fine scrambled egg. Gently mix the egg into the second portion of Basic Sushi Rice and divide it among four cocktail glasses (or other serving dishes).

5. Garnish each with a sprig of chervil or parsley.

6. To make the Cheese-mopolitan sushi, gently mix the diced cucumber, tomatoes and cheese into the third portion of Basic Sushi Rice.

7. Divide the rice among four cocktail glasses (or other serving dishes).

CONCLUSION

Sushi has become a global phenomenon: sushi restaurants today can be found in cities all around the world, and they each have created their own version of a millennia of history, like the many sushi "fusion" restaurants attest.

Thanks to its evolution millions of people are able enjoy sushi in all its shiny culinary heritage. However, it is important to recognize the cultural significance of this traditional Japanese dish and to respect the techniques and traditions that have been passed down through the generations.

Whether enjoyed in a traditional sushi restaurant in Japan or at a casual sushi bar abroad, sushi is a delicious and deeply ingrained part of Japanese culture that continues to be enjoyed by people all over the world.

I really hope you have found much value inside this book, as I have put in it the love I have for my culture and the Japanese cuisine. If you have found any great recipe that you are now proud to make for your loved ones, please take few minutes from your day and leave a review in the website where you purchased the book from.

Follow me on social media and subscribe to my newsletter if you want to receive updates on my future projects, additional recipes, and a chance to have free copies of my new books!

With love,

Sarah Otagawa

INDEX

Barbecue Hot Dog Sushi Roll	77
Barbecued pork inside-out rolls	76
Beef celery sushi rice salad	78
Brown Rice Quinoa Sushi Rolls	107
Brown rice smoked salmon rolls	35
Buffalo Chicken Sushi	79
Butternut Squash Rolls	105
California Roll Sushi	30
Cauliflower Rice Sushi Bowls	108
Cauliflower Rice Sushi Bowls with Tofu	109
Cauliflower Tuna Sushi Rolls	46
Chicken Salad Sushi	81
Chicken Sushi	82
Chicken Sushi Delicacy	100
Chicken rice sushi	80
Chickpea Salad Sushi Wrap	110
Chili Rice Bowl with Beef & Egg	101
Cocktail sushi	132
Cocktail sushi	38
Crab and avocado sushi	31
Crab stick salad canapé	31
Crab stick salad canapé	39
Cream Cheese & Crab Rolls	40
Crispy Tofu Sushi Burrito	111
Cucumber Sushi Rolls	104
Cucumber sushi parcels + salmon	41
Curry Salmon Sushi Stacks	42
Easy salmon sushi rice bowl	27
Eggplant sushi	115
Fig & Coconut Dessert Sushi	128
Fruit Sushi Rice	127
Full Sea Sushi	50
Furikake Sushi Casserole	114
Green Sushi w/ Fresh Goat Cheese	87
Grilled Bacon Sushi Roll	83
Grilled eel sushi	43
Homemade Vegan Sushi Rolls + Quinoa	117
Inside-Out Spicy Tuna & Avo Sushi	44
Japanese omelet sushi	45
Key Lime Dessert Sushi	131
Korean Kimchi Sushi Rolls	84
Maki Sushi with Baked Fish	47
Maki and Nigiri Sushi	22
Maki and Nigiri Sushi	24
ngo & Curry Salmon Stacks + Rice	48
o Sushi Bowl	118
ted Fish Sushi	49
ed Tuna Hand Rolls	36
me Dipping Sauce	119
oll / Shrimp, avocado, cucumber	33
l / Seafood medley	29
	85
om and Chicken Sushi	95
Paella Sushi	51
Peking Duck Sushi	88
Pink Sushi	89
Pork Cutlet Tonkatsu Sushi	90
Prosciutto Rolls	92
Quinoa Sushi Rolls w/	119
Restaurant-style Raw Fish Sushi	53
Rice & Quinoa Prawn Sushi Bowl	52
Roast Beef Asparagus Rolls	93
Roasted Sweet Potato Sushi	121
Salmon Roe Canapé	39
Salmon Sushi Salad	54
Seared Tataki Beef Sushi	94
Shrimp Rice Pilaf Sushi	58
Shrimp Rolls	59
Shrimp Sushi	60
Shrimp and Salmon Sushi Rolls	55
Simple Smoked Salmon Sushi	32
Smoked Duck Sushi w/ Orange	91
Smoked Mackerel Maki Rolls	61
Smoked Salmon Canapé	62
Smoked Salmon Sushi Roll	63
Spicy Crab Roll	64
Spicy Tuna Sesame Roll	57
Spicy Tuna Sushi Roll	66
Stir Fry Noodles with Shrimps	112
Stir Fry Noodles with Shrimps	23
Sushi Burrito Bowl	120
Sushi Crab Salad Recipe	67
Sushi Eel Eggrolls w/ Cream Cheese	68
Sushi Spaghetti Salad	37
Sweet Chili Chicken Sushi	96
Sweet Potato Tempura & Avocado Rolls	122
Sweet Sushi w/ Kiwi Rhubarb	130
Sweet Sushi with Chocolate	129
Taco sushi	97
Teriyaki Chicken Pouches Sushi	98
Teriyaki Chicken Sushi Roll	99
Thai Shrimp Sushi Parcels	69
Tofu & Mushroom Kimbap Wrap	124
Tokyo-style Sushi Rice Salad	70
Traditional Nori Tuna Rolls	71
Tuna Avocado Sushi Rice Salad	65
Tuna Delight Nigiri	28
Tuna Delight Nigiri	34
Tuna Fillet Rice Salad	73
Tuna Salad Rolls	72
Tuna Tartare Gunkan Sushi	74
Two-cheese Tuna Salad Rolls	75
Vegan Sushi Bowl w/ Sesame Soy Dressing	125
Vegan Sushi Bowls	106
Vegan Sushi Burrito w/ Air Fryer Tofu	113
Vegan Sushi Sandwich	126
Veggie Sushi	103
Yakitori Sushi Skewers	102
Soft-Shell Crab Sushi Roll	62

Printed in Great Britain
by Amazon